AHA!

Method Book

A Socially and Emotionally Intelligent
Approach to Working with Teenagers

By
Jennifer Freed, Ph.D., MFT
Edited by Melissa Lynn Lowenstein

Table of Contents

Who We Are/What We Do

AHA! is a social-emotional learning (SEL) program founded in 1999 by Jennifer Freed, PhD and Rendy Freedman, MFT. The program's mission is to develop character, social-emotional intelligence, imagination, and social conscience in teenagers, and to prevent bullying by building healthy connections across lines of clique, color, and socioeconomic status.

Facilitators applying AHA!'s unique method support teens in learning to:

- Express themselves healthfully and creatively
- Appreciate diversity
- Empathize and work with others
- Set and meet goals
- Engage in school
- Solve problems
- Listen empathically
- Speak and act with integrity
- Be responsible
- Create healthy relationships
- Be of service to the community
- Help rid school environments of bullying, violence, prejudice, sexism, and racism

The AHA! Method is not an extra set of lessons to teach, but a way of working with youth. It is experiential, action-and discussion-based. It is an approach to cooperative learning that involves students in games, activities, and facilitated discussions.

This manual offers skills to youth providers that facilitate mutualistic and socially/emotionally intelligent relationships with and between youth. Whether you are a teacher, a school administrator, a therapist, a parent, or out-of-school program provider, the AHA! Method will help you create environments of collaborative learning and sharing. It sets out guidelines for being the kind of adult role model and mentor young people need: compassionate, empathic, authoritative (rather than authoritarian), well-boundaried, curious, socially conscious, and easy to relate to.

AHA!'s out-of-school groups provide a place to delve deeply into personal issues and sensitive material. Youth in these programs spend an hour and a half to two hours together each week for 12-13 weeks. Trust and vulnerability unfold organically. In-school groups don't process as deeply; groups are larger and AHA! facilitators spend only an hour with each group once per week for 6-10 weeks. In-school programs focus more on content and on building initial connections between students who might otherwise not connect.

As you read through this book and decide how to apply the AHA! method, consider factors like these: Do youth you work with have enough time together as a group to build closeness and trust? If they do, you can explore more sensitive material. If you are working in a normal school classroom setting, expect to maintain a less vulnerable conversation. As a facilitator, you have the privilege of setting the tone.

The Importance of a High Staff to Participant Ratio

Having a high staff to participant ratio of six to eight participants to one facilitator is an important part of the AHA! Method. It sends a powerful non-verbal message that participants are valuable and that we, as adults, care enough about their future to get involved. A high staff-to-student ratio also increases the safety of the program. With more trained adult facilitators, we can attend more to the needs of each participant. It becomes less likely that any one teen with a major problem could slip through the cracks of our awareness.

Although students may have one or two important teachers over the course of their schooling, increasing class sizes tend to make close and confiding student-teacher relationships more the exception than the rule. Teachers are often constrained by their busy schedules and the nature of their roles as evaluators. Similarly, working parents, who are frequently stretched to their limits by job and family demands, rarely have the luxury of spending afternoon hours engaging in activities and conversations with their children. Having a high staff-to-youth ratio in an after-school or in-school program creates a rare opportunity for the formation of strong intergenerational ties.

A high ratio of staff to students:

- Exposes teens to varying adult influences and perspectives, which they can use as guiding forces in their own growth and development.

- Creates an environment where youth have more options to reach out for and receive adult guidance.
- Makes limit-setting, monitoring, and control easier.
- Creates greater potential for checks and balances within the culture of the staff.

All this being said, having a lower ratio in the classroom or out-of-school program isn't always possible. If this is the case for you, the guidelines and concepts laid out in these pages will still have value.

Why We Do What We Do

The competencies created through the AHA! Method create a community of socially and emotionally intelligent contributors. Teens guided to their best selves through this program are well prepared for happy, accomplished adult lives.

A growing evidence base supports the importance of social-emotional intelligence (resilience, emotional management, capacity for empathy, teamwork, initiative, and problem solving) in creating happiness and health. Most scholars and policymakers agree that because these essential skills enable us to interact effectively and harmoniously with other people, they may be more essential than academics as predictors of success in later life.

Greater investment in school, improved test scores, reduced bullying and violence, and reduced disciplinary referrals and suspensions are some of the results you can expect with teens exposed to the AHA! Method.

One of the most important impacts of the AHA! Method is prevention of bullying and cruel behavior. Any involvement in bullying – whether as a victim, a witness, or a perpetrator – is associated with negative outcomes like poor school performance, substance abuse, and suicidal or delinquent behavior. One study of over 2,000 students aged 12-16 found that those who witnessed bullying reported more feelings of depression, anxiety, hostility, and inferiority than the bullies or victims. Rather than approaching this issue with the idea that people with bullying behaviors can only be stopped through punitive means or by being separated from their communities, AHA! creates an environment inhospitable to bullying or cruel behavior as it knits teens together through connecting activities, vulnerable sharing, deep listening, collaborative learning, play, and creativity.

Over 30 percent of young people aged 12-17 report depression or depression-related feelings, where they feel so sad or hopeless every day for two weeks or more that they stop doing some usual activities. Anxiety is an equally urgent issue that impacts young people's health and well-being. Social-emotional learning programs like AHA! have been found to enhance teen mental health. Students who feel less connected to their schools more often report depression-related feelings; students who feel accepted at school are more highly motivated, engaged in learning, and committed to benefiting from their educational experience. Teens in AHA! programs report:

- Improvement in multiple problematic areas of their lives
- Improvement in their ability to accept others without judgment
- Reduced likelihood that they will do things that are hurtful to others
- Improved ability to intervene peacefully in bullying and conflict situations

American Educational Research Association. (2013). Prevention of bullying in schools, colleges, and universities: Research report and recommendations. Retrieved from: http://www.aera.net/Publications/Books/PreventionofBullying. Hertz, M. F., et al. (2013). Bullying and suicide: A public health approach. Journal of Adolescent Health, 53(1), S1-S3. Retrieved from: http://www.jahonline.org/article/S1054-139X%2813%2900270-X/fulltext. National Center for Injury Prevention and Control, Centers for Disease Control and Prevention. (2014). The relationship between bullying and suicide: What we know and what it means for schools. Retrieved from: http://www.cdc.gov/violenceprevention/pdf/bullying-suicide-translation-final-a.pdf

- Less likelihood they will use hurtful language, and confidence that they have tools to peacefully confront use of this kind of language by others
- Improved campus climate
- More joy

Part One

How To Facilitate

Facilitate (v.): To make it possible or easier for something to happen.

Facilitator (n.): one that helps to bring about an outcome (as learning, productivity, or communication) by providing indirect or unobtrusive assistance, guidance, or supervision.

Guidelines For Facilitation

We use the word *facilitator* to describe a person delivering the AHA! Method. This word was chosen carefully to represent the true function of the person or people who do this work. They act not as authority figures handing down wisdom, but as gentle, well-boundaried, reliable sources of guidance, supervision, and support.

Although a facilitator is more a role model than a teacher, teachers can also be facilitators. Youth program leaders, therapists, and administrators can too. It's more about a mindset than a job description – an idea that the facilitator's role is to provide structure and inspiration that will allow youth to feel ownership of their own experience.

It is the responsibility of facilitators to create and foster what we call a "safe container" in which students feel safe to connect, express themselves, and receive new ideas with curiosity and engagement. These facilitation guidelines are meant to help you to show up as an adult who is supportive, fun, and curious, and who recognizes that teens thrive best in a connected community, not an authoritarian regime.

Prioritize staff self-care.

At AHA!, we place a high priority on self-care. At each staff meeting during check-in, attendees offer up a self-care score between 1 and 10. A high score means we are eating nutritious food, getting adequate sleep and exercise, having regular downtime to re-charge, and having regular opportunities for creative expression.

It is easy as a youth provider to overwork and over-extend one's self. The needs of those we serve can seem vast; well-meaning helpers may end up sacrificing their own well-being by working too hard or failing to take adequate time and focus for good self-care.

Service to youth *requires* excellent self-care. If we don't care for ourselves adequately, the stresses we face in this work can not only damage our own health and well-being, but can also make us less able to work well with young people. Setting an example of burning the candle at both ends does not serve youth well, either.

Organizations should avoid overworking their staff and should offer reflective downtime as part of the job. Without these elements, staff attrition and unhealthy staff members are guaranteed. It's better to slow things down and plan for staff retreats and staff morale days than to cram staff hours to overflowing and expect productivity. Productivity without joy and inspiration is just sweat equity. It won't translate to charismatic, capable, calm adults – which is what teens need to see.

Staff leader Ringo knows that if he comes to group with a smirk and a growl – which is what he feels like doing, since he's feeling overworked and overwhelmed – teens will think it's okay to come to sessions with a bad attitude. He realizes that he has been shirking on his own self-care and is suffering the consequences, and asks Felicia for a few minutes of her staff time beforehand. He uses that time with her to talk through his issues, make a doable plan for self-care for the rest of the week, and promises to be accountable to Felicia about following through on his plan. They take a few seconds to "tap in" Ringo's positive intentions (see below). At check-in, he shares about this experience, helping the teens learn that adults can struggle and succeed at resetting their "'tude" into a positive plan.

This being said, stressed and cranky staff members are a fact of life, because self-care is not always easy to balance with life's demands. We aren't trying to appear unflappable to teens – we're modeling resiliency and good coping skills, not perfection. In times when stress is high and moods are sour, staff members are responsible for self-care that will maintain the safety and integrity of group life. If a staff member feels "off" or is in a bad mood, it's up to him or her to handle it outside of the group.

Tapping-In

Self-care can be extraordinarily simple. On a day when you feel challenged and cranky, taking even a simple, brief step to improve your mood and attitude can make all the difference. As you care for yourself in this way, you make yourself more available to collaborate and do thoughtful deeds for others. One way to do this is to engage in a process called "tapping-in."

Laurel Parnell, a therapist who is a well-known expert in the field of EMDR (Eye Movement Desensitization and Reprocessing) has developed a simple method for "tapping in" positive memories, thoughts, and imaginings, which she calls Resource Tapping. In AHA!, we use tapping-in often as a staff and we teach it to youth we serve.

1. Find a comfortable place to sit or lie, where you will not be disturbed. Close your eyes.
2. Take several long, slow breaths, fill the belly, and exhale

slowly. Let yourself relax.

3. Imagine any type of positive state: being peaceful, happy, inspired, motivated, or laughing. This can be called up based on your actual experience – somewhere you've been, or an event from your past – or can be drawn from your imagination as an experience you wish to have. (An imagined experience, seen in detail, can have just as much positive impact as a real one.)

Suggested Positive States for Tapping

Happily surprised

Motivated

Comforted by someone

Excited

Grateful

Cared about

Inspired

Laughing hard

Doing something brave

Completing something you worked hard at

Feeling really relaxed

Feeling open to a new experience

Something really good has just happened

You loved an animal or something in nature

You did something wonderful for someone – even a small thing

Someone gave you a gift you loved

Someone took the time to listen to you

Once you have an association, bring up as much sensory detail as you can: sights, sounds, smells, sensations, and the emotional feeling that goes with being there. You might even imagine the

12

time of year, the time of day, and what you are wearing in this special place. Check in to feel where in your body you most experience this image, feeling, or sound.

4.   When you have a sense of the place, begin to tap on your knees right-left, right-left. The taps can be quick or slow; find a speed that feels good to you. Do this six to 12 times (tapping right and left equals one time). Alternatively, you can do 'butterfly taps,' crossing your arms in front of your chest and tapping your right upper arm with your left hand and your left upper arm with your right hand.

5. Pause; check in with yourself to see how you are feeling.

6. You may keep tapping as long as it feels positive.

Repeat as often as you like.

If you have any problem following the instructions above, search for "Laurel Parnell Resource Tapping" on YouTube for video instructions.

Prepare thoroughly, but adhere to the 50/50 rule.

Plan curriculum for 100 percent of a group while maintaining the flexibility to disregard 50 percent of it to make space for what is alive in the room and pertinent to address. Plan appropriate curriculum that is engaging, meaningful, easy to instruct, well thought out, and applicable to your audience.

Take whatever time is needed to prepare for a group that has ease and flow and that is accessible to everyone in attendance. This preparation time will vary from day to day, group to group, and facilitator to facilitator. Things to consider are:

- The time required to present each segment of whatever content you intend to introduce.

- Possible questions that may arise during the presentation and how you might address them either before or after they are asked.

- How you want to arrange the room to best meet the needs of the day's topic and participants.

- How to best facilitate the ideal environment for learning and engaging, depending on the size of the group; for example, consider whether you'll need to break into smaller groups for some parts of the lesson.

Even with all this forethought and planning, be prepared for whatever might need to be addressed in the moment, and don't over-prepare. Stay on your toes to avoid losing your audience or simply mowing over someone's needs or desires so that you can "stay on task" and teach rigidly according to an agenda. Have the flexibility to factor what is happening in the room into the presentation. This brings what you are teaching to life. We may not get to everything on our curriculum list for the day, but we have a greater opportunity to engage with our audience - and we are less likely to become rote or stale.

Plan for the space in which you will be working.

Know the space you will be working within. Get as good an idea as possible of any limitations you'll encounter in terms of space, layout, seating and sound quality. Whatever the space you're given, make sure to be explicit about the benefits or challenges of that space and involve the teens in figuring out the best way to make it work.

Sometimes we have no control over the space in which we teach. However, we should do everything we can to create spaces that allow for the teen brain to reach and discover – to feel free and imaginative.

Facilitators Tricia and Daniel are only able to get a rectangular hallway to work within, because all classrooms are taken. They end up planning their curriculum to make use of pushing up to walls, facing off in long lines and creating ways to "do-si-do" with their lesson plans.

Get physical.

A didactic presentation with no movement or visual/kinesthetic aids will almost always lose teens' attention. Teenagers need to be physical, so incorporate fun physicality throughout group meetings. Plan lessons where teens sit and listen only for short periods. Include games where youth get to move in a bigger way, as well as smaller kinesthetic elements: for example, turning to a partner for brief "pair and share" conversations, or asking for a show of hands from students in response to an aspect of the lesson or another student's sharing.

Attend to timing and flow.

Create lessons that allow participants to enter the flow easily and gently. Once they are engaged, do your best to maintain flow and tempo. Give them the experience of being in the flow and enjoying it. Provide opportunities for small wins or personal accomplishments along the way.

Don't try to be the expert, even if you are one.

The information or insights you have to offer may be useful, but temper them with your own "beginner's mind." A facilitator entering with the attitude of a student will build trust and rapport more quickly with youth and will learn as much as he or she teaches!

Participate fully in all activities.

AHA!'s method is based on a relational model, not the authoritarian model found in most classrooms. Show up as a participant. Talk with, not at. AHA! makes frequent use of a circle format, which helps foster a sense that everyone in the room is an active, equal participant. Avoid standing in the middle of the circle to lecture to students; instead, speak from your spot in the circle. Get used to the idea of teaching as a circle participant. If you need to present something didactic, break up the circle and set up a white board or other visual aid.

Be an excellent listener.

Your ability to listen non-judgmentally is crucial to creating a safe container. Here are some points and pointers to keep in mind as you cultivate listening skills.

- Make eye contact when culturally appropriate.
- Show interest by active listening, nodding or saying "uh-

huh."

- Allow for pauses; be patient.
- Give your full attention; stop other tasks.
- Show understanding and connection: "I understand." "I see."
- Attempt to identify the underlying feelings: "It sounds like you felt disappointed..." "How did you feel when...?"
- Clarify and paraphrase, particularly the feelings: "So, you really felt insulted, is that it?"
- Empathize: "That must be hard for you to feel that."
- Remain neutral and relaxed; try not to imply judgment or disapproval through body language or facial expressions.
- Help the person focus while showing interest: "What bothered you the most about it?" or "What did you like the most?"
- Don't spend your time preparing your response. Focus on the speaker.
- Don't interrupt, evaluate or jump to conclusions.
- Focus on feelings, not facts.
- Avoid "scene stealing," advising, fixing, interrogating, correcting or debating.

Remember that authentically listening will help others feel heard, understood, valued, respected and cared for.

Be authentic, honest, and vulnerable.

If you are nervous, say so...it will help everyone. Speak freely about your emotions.

Don't over-share.

Facilitators should share with discernment. Don't share personal stories, dramas or crises that will cause participants to want to take care of you. Take these stories, dramas and crises to trusted adults for feedback and support. Only share what you know to be in the best interests of the youth.

Engage the playful, curious side of yourself with enthusiasm.

Playfulness and enthusiasm are contagious. Do what's necessary to show up with these qualities as often as you can.

Be aware of context, culture, and audience when planning activities, and be willing to improvise/regroup where you encounter surprises.

Context and culture underpin the buy-in and experience of any group. Show up prepared with an understanding of the actual hardscape of the place in which you will be working, and with an understanding of the people you will be serving on that day. Know the age, customs, slang, unspoken social order and issues of the people who will be participating in your group. Ask yourself:

- **How are these participants likely to feel about the information I am sharing?** Consider what you might expect in terms of reaction, cooperation and attention. Preparing in this way will help you troubleshoot and to avoid being thrown off by participants' responses.
- **How can I make this fun and encourage all in this particular group to participate?** Learning and connection

happen more easily among people who are enjoying themselves! Make an effort to instill plenty of fun into the activities you design, keeping in mind the nature of the group you'll be working and playing with. Creating a sense of fun is usually as simple as including one of the interactive games described later in this book.

Always be prepared to troubleshoot when you have limited information ahead of time.

Ben is hired to work within a private academy of a public high school. The administrative component of that school is incredibly supportive and warm. But when Ben shows up with his team, he finds that students haven't been informed about the program or even that they would be coming in to work with them that day, so they enter the room late and confused. The youth are also 99 percent Caucasian and mostly upper middle class. The room, the confusion, and the attitudes throw Ben off.

After an awkward first day, Ben regroups and asks the administrator to make sure that the next group meeting is held in a private, undisturbed location; that a teacher from the school be present to support his efforts; and that students have plenty of notice about AHA! days. He then reorganizes curriculum based on privilege challenges rather than oppression issues. He corrects his own attitudes about the seemingly arrogant postures of the students, and realizes that their issues of self-worth, bullying and character are just as vital and challenging as those of as any obviously oppressed group.

Model what you teach.

Facilitators are expected to model the concepts and processes taught here in their relationships with faculty and participants alike. Lead through development of mutual trust, respect and agreement.

Set guidelines, not rules.

In the AHA! Method, we establish guidelines for the group's behavior as a group. We do this as soon as the group begins to meet, and revisit these guidelines as needed throughout ongoing sessions.

Developmentally, teens need to contest authority. Most teens are inflamed by hard, authoritarian rules. Many teens believe rules are meant to be broken. Rules are typically established by an outside source, which can feel oppressive to youth. They can be seen as impositions of adults onto children and are often dictated for control; guidelines are developed in community for everyone's safety, cohesion, and nourishment. They are perceived as mutually agreed-upon boundaries for group life and incorporate everybody's input about what is right for them.

Carla starts the workshop group by asking participants: "What agreements do we need to make to create safety and a close, trustworthy community?" Participants eagerly express needs for punctuality, confidentiality, kindness, sobriety and other desirable qualities. As Carla and her co-facilitators guide them, participants feel empowered and listened to. Carla is especially careful to address confidentiality: what group members can and cannot share with others who are not members of the group. Other agreements are made as the group calls for them and agrees upon them. She writes their responses on a whiteboard. Together, the group uses them to craft the guidelines they will all follow when they are together.

Rules do have their place, especially when safety is involved. Rules may be necessary, for example, to prevent physical violence, bullying, or destruction of property.

Re-think discipline.

When misbehavior or disrespect emerges, it's tempting for the adults in the room to pull rank and lay down the law. This is one surefire way to sabotage the essence of this method. It creates cooperation based in fear and will often alienate participants who, ultimately, are the most in need of adult support and mentorship.

This is a non-hierarchical model. We are committed to avoiding the "power-over" role of the disciplinarian. Where discipline is needed, we adhere to a restorative model, where inappropriate behavior and negative attitudes are generally seen as a group issue. See acting-out as an opportunity to teach participants how to deal with feelings that arise in response to inappropriate behavior – whether they are the source of, a victim of, or a witness to that behavior. This is how we guide students in learning and practicing conflict management skills.

When misbehavior occurs, restorative approaches dictate the evaluation of the cause, effect and emotions as a group. Together, the group then searches for the appropriate action.

Where appropriate, AHA! facilitators model looking beyond the behavior to address its stimulus. A restorative approach is always

21

more effective than authoritarianism and punishment. It models compassionate action and engenders mutual trust and respect. It creates not fear-based compliance, but an internalized wish to get along and to participate in community. (Dr. Beverly Title's book *Teaching Peace* is a comprehensive resource on restorative approaches: http://resolutionariesinc.com/teaching-peace-book/)

See mistakes as opportunities for learning.

Acknowledgment of mistakes and learning to make them a natural part of the life process is intrinsic to the AHA! model. Mistakes made by facilitators or participants should be acknowledged and addressed not as things that should never have happened, but as opportunities for learning, growth and connection.

Agreement on the issue is not the point. Acknowledgment of others' experience is. Model empathy for the experience of the person giving feedback. Consider it deeply within yourself. Ask participants, "If I could've acted differently, what would that look like?" Facilitators' willingness to accept feedback from students sets an essential tone for the group's willingness to embrace and learn from mistakes. Practice looking past defensiveness for kernels of truth. Express gratitude for the feedback being given.

Set and maintain the "container."

Setting the container refers to creating a safe space in which youth can dare to be vulnerable. Maintain that space as the group unfolds by: (1) monitoring the depth and pace of the process, and (2) influencing that depth and pace where necessary.

Juan, the lead facilitator, begins group by reviewing confidentiality. He highlights how essential this agreement is to the creation of a safe mutual space in which group members can share vulnerably. His tone is slow, heartfelt and measured. He makes eye contact with youth as he speaks. Here, he is working to create a safe container marked by calmness, depth and an invitation to share deeply. As the group unfolds, Andrea, the process facilitator, helps hold the ground of this deeper container by asking deepening, open-ended follow-up questions.

Use what is in the room.

Know that at times, even the best-planned lesson can turn out to be a flop because it lacks meaning or relevance to the group being served. Things often change in the moment depending on the mood of the group or the particulars of the school or community.

Come to group with a general plan, but don't become so rigid that you cannot deviate from it when this is called for. Always be prepared to shift gears to respond to participant needs. One example might be sharing by a participant of sensitive or difficult personal information. If this occurs during a game, facilitators can ask the group whether they would appreciate the opportunity to address issues brought up rather than continuing with the activity. This can then be done in the form of a Connection Circle, a format frequently used in the AHA! Method that is covered in detail in a later section of this book. Unscheduled Connection Circles deepen connections and lend support to the disclosing participant.

Brendan is leading a discussion on communication with a group of high school youth. The students seem checked out and bored. He stops the discussion and asks the group, "Does this topic we're looking at impact you?" He states what he sees. "People seem like they're not connecting to this conversation...What's going on for you all today?" One of the teens shares that a student at her school killed herself yesterday. Now, Brendan and his co-facilitators understand why the energy was so low. They take this opportunity to turn the group into a source of support for the grieving teens.

Be spontaneous.

Spontaneity is a quality of staying in the present moment and acting and reacting improvisationally from a place of authenticity and integrity. Planning is good, as is a firm intention regarding what the group will be doing; and it is also important to be willing to let things take an unexpected turn – often, that's where the really good conversations happen.

During a meeting, allow whatever comes up to dictate the group's direction. Go with the skid, not against it. Don't get too attached to staying on track or sticking with your pre-planned curriculum. Pay attention to cues from each group member and let your response steer the group into unexpected places. Be spontaneous.

Randi is presenting to a group of 25 teens on how to clearly communicate frustration to parents without judging them or making them wrong. During her presentation, a teen rolls his eyes, lets out a sighing moan, and then begins to whisper to his neighbor. Randi has a lot to teach that day, but sees an opportunity to use what is in the room as a living example of what she is teaching. Instead of moving past it, she turns and incorporates it into her day's lesson plan. "Johnny, it seems like you have something to say and I am interested in your feedback."
"This is stupid," Johnny replies. "This would never work at my house. My dad never listens to me."

"That sounds incredibly frustrating."

"It is..." Johnny goes on to talk about his relationship with his father, which helps him engage and deepens the whole group's experience of the lesson. As Randi listens intently and helps Johnny express what is alive in him, she also weaves in other participants who empathize with Johnny's experience. Together, they explore how they might use their actual situations and feelings to incorporate what Randi is teaching in a meaningful way.

Listen, watch and otherwise sense what's going on at the surface, but also attend to any subtexts or energies running below that surface. If you sense that the activity wants to take a novel direction, allow this to happen while maintaining a strong container.

Also be willing to follow your intuitive sense of when it's time to re-assert the day's or the activity's intention when the group's energy becomes too scattered or negative. This, too, is a way of being spontaneous. If Johnny's problem has nothing to do with the day's presentation, you may choose to find a way to acknowledge and compartmentalize it so that the group isn't sidetracked completely.

Allow for silence.

We need more reflective time in our amped-up, speedy, loud world. In a culture that over-appreciates loudness and talkativeness, it is essential to cultivate a climate of welcoming the reflective and contemplative as equally alive and participatory. Teaching youth about the contribution of quiet witnessing brings much more animation to the diversity of sharing styles in the room.

Fernando says he is not ready to talk about the topic. Martin, the facilitator, thanks him for his honesty and acknowledges how well Fernando is listening and giving his attention to others. Fernando feels recognized and appreciated and starts to pay even more attention in the group. Later, he takes a risk by sharing.

Participants who tend to be on the quiet side need to feel important and valued. The more we pressure introverted types to share in large groups, the more they will feel wrong and inadequate. When someone is shut down or quiet, the worst thing we can do is shame them for that; this will only drive them deeper into their bubble. It is always best to attempt to see what is behind the behavior. This is what ultimately will help bring out the young person's authentic expression of him or herself. When the group is silent after a facilitator asks a question, allow time; no need to jump in and rescue.

Show, don't tell.

Sharing information creates knowledge. Sharing experiences creates wisdom. Teens need both, of course. However: they are in a developmental period of experimentation. Being a teen means testing your capacities and boundaries. Felt experiences have more of an imprinting effect than memorizing data. Lessons that are embodied rather than taught will create more connection to the teens.

Tom saw that many teens were getting in their own way with excessive self-criticism. To help them with this, he devised an exercise he called "Kicks In the Head." He had each teen describe five different ways their inner critic kicks

them in the head. Then, he had the teens externalize those voices by having
other teens say them, then brainstorm ways to deal with those negative internal
states. All the teens could relate. They started to strategize ways to get through
those negative "kicks" to a more proactive, supported state of mind.

Don't hand out a fact sheet about a sensitive, important subject like teen pregnancy or family violence, then test teens on content without any discussion or inquiry into their own knowledge or wisdom about the subject in question. The entire group's experiences can be considered a petri dish of successful and failed experiments. Get the teens interested in their own findings and support them in making the most of their lessons.

Address different learning styles.

We cannot teach to all students in the same way. We need to bring topics to life for all kinds of learners: auditory, kinesthetic, and visual. Some of us embody a combination of two or all three.

Robbie is not following the lecture Jennifer is giving on managing emotions. He
asks repetitive questions. He is not getting it. Jennifer is frustrated because
Robbie is holding others back from learning. She then realizes that Robbie,
like so many others, is not an auditory learner. He is a kinesthetic learner who
learns by doing. So Jennifer asks the group how to put what she is talking
about into a physical practice or exercise. The group decides that they need to
have emotional management teams who come up with ways to work with
different emotions. Then they role-play their findings to the group.

As facilitators, we provide content suitable for all three kinds of learners. Address the learning styles of everyone in the room. Keep in mind that you are a particular kind of learner yourself; don't get stuck repeating your own comfortable style of disseminating information in ways that might leave others out of the learning.

Be play-centered; keep humor in the picture.

Play is in the heart of any joyful human being. A joyous, laughter-filled approach to learning draws teens toward vitality and creativity in a world that can sometimes seem grim and oppressive.

Rena is talking about some family challenges. Ryan goes to hug Rena and she accidentally elbows Ryan in the nose. Rena starts laughing uncontrollably, which starts a contagion of laughing all around the room. The facilitator also starts laughing and says, "It's so great that even when we're having a rough day, we can remember that it is okay to release into laughter."

Lightening up doesn't mean not going deep. It means prioritizing levity over somberness and righteousness. Engaging teens in a curious and playful attitude towards serious subjects can lessen their anxiety and help them to become calm and focused.

Scolding teens for laughter where it seems inappropriate may make them comply, but they will feel disengaged. Instead of barking at teens Brian and Briana when one plays with the other's hair during group, Ben, the facilitator, could gently say, "I so appreciate your affection, but let's bring it back." The teens might be a little embarrassed, but they will willingly bring their attention back to Ben.

A facilitator who can laugh at him or herself is a facilitator that teens will trust. With teens' raging hormones and the ever-unpredictable flows of group life, humor is a saving grace.

When confronted with the odd behaviors, dramatic twists and scary turns that are inevitable with teens, it's essential for facilitators to remain detached enough to see the absurdity factor. If you take yourself too seriously, teenagers will consistently find ways to puncture your veneer. Don't use shame, sarcasm, or teasing in any form to create group shift.

Choose cultural empathy over political correctness.

To be culturally empathic means to tune into the group you are serving rather than showing up with a preconceived idea of how people should talk or share. Each group has its language norms and styles. It is best to listen for those nuances and appreciate them for what they are instead of enforcing a language code that could shut down authentic sharing.

In his check-in at group, Brady shares that he's happy because David was his "beee-yatch" today and helped him with all his homework. Facilitator Aaron waits until everyone has checked in before asking, with real curiosity, "What does that word 'beee-yatch' mean to you all? How do you feel when you hear it?" This – and Aaron's commitment to being non-reactive to and curious about a term that he personally finds offensive – leads to a juicy conversation about how words hurt or help, and how they affect people differently. Brady learns that some folks in the room feel really hurt by that phrase and that his casual use of it may need reconsideration.

Rather than holding a rigid expectation about how each individual should share, open up the conversation to spontaneous expression that isn't limited by preconceived "shoulds."

If your working environment prohibits challenging language, you may find it necessary to gently redirect students who use such language; but if at all possible, don't shut down genuine sharing only because it contains challenging language. You may shut a student down right at the point where he or she has summoned the courage to share about something important.

Aggressive language or truly offensive language, on the other hand, does not need to be tolerated, but can be redirected: "You seem angry, but it isn't okay to use that kind of language to hurt someone else." Take the focus back to the real source of the anger, which is almost never the person being targeted in the room.

Practice positive framing when working with distractions.

We create the frame of students' experiences in AHA! through the ways we comment on their words and actions. It's paramount to positively frame students' words and actions as much as possible.

Pedro says, "I am really bored right now." The facilitator responds, "Pedro, you are so great to bring up the need to switch things up because you want to be more involved." Jolene says, "My mother never lets me do anything. She is so mean." The facilitator responds, "Your mom sounds like she really wants to make sure you are safe and protected. Tell us why she might have those concerns." A facilitator sees that many youth are acting distracted and antsy. She says, "It seems like there is extra energy today. We all need to figure out how to use it to get the most out of today's subject. Let's brainstorm some ways to use this energy."

In moments where negativity threatens to override the learning environment, actively seek out ways to create positive frames through which all can view the current situation or the material being shared.

Don't buy into negative frames. If Bobby says he never does anything right, and Julie says, "Well, that's because you never try – DUH," and the facilitator adds, more gently, "Bobby, it does seem like you don't put in much effort," Bobby ends up feeling helpless and like a loser. Instead, the facilitator might say to Bobby, "It seems like you want to do better at some things in your life. How can Julie and the rest of us help you make the first step on one of those things you care about?"

Promptly share and repair problems between group leaders.

Co-leaders will have tensions and disagreements. Any negative conversation carried on in one person's head about another will cause relationship harm if left unshared and unresolved. Make a habit of taking time to check in with your co- leaders about things you can both improve.

Ted and Jan meet after group regularly to discuss how they can better co-lead. One day, Ted says to Jan, "I would like you to interrupt me less. I would like more time to get my point across." Jan replies, "Great…I will do that. Can you work on being more animated when you talk, and looking more at the youth? Sometimes your voice is quite flat, and you look up at the ceiling a lot when you talk to them." Ted replies that he knows he does this, thanks Jan for the reminder, and says he will be working on that.

Facilitators should use "I-statements" about their positions: "Brad, I want to share with you that in our work together, sometimes I don't have as much of a voice in what we do or how the session

31

goes…and I notice that you aren't open to my feedback. Can we talk this over?" This kind of emotional hygiene and co-facilitator honesty leads to dynamic, cohesive group leadership.

Model and express gratitude.

Gratitude is the state of being grateful, thankful, or appreciative. When working with youth, it is useful to share gratitude for one another, ourselves, and life in general. This is especially helpful in the face of ever-increasing demands on organizations who serve youth and on the youth who participate. At AHA!, we close every group with a round of brief gratitude statements.

At the end of one group meeting, facilitator Fatima says, "Let's go around the circle and hear from everyone. Share one thing you are feeling grateful for right now in your life. I'll start." She shares about a small success in her life, helping illustrate to the teens that there is always something to be grateful for, no matter how challenging life may seem. Her co-facilitators and participants go around the circle, sharing and listening. Those who would rather not share are allowed to pass. After the circle completes, Fatima makes sure to return once more to those who passed to give them a chance to share.

People who practice gratitude take better care of themselves, exercise more, and have healthier diets. Gratitude has been shown to help with stress and anxiety management and to boost immune system function, benefit sleep, and increase optimism. Gratitude has been shown to lead to higher long-term satisfaction with life, including kinder behaviors towards others and less aggressive behaviors in response to provocation.

Without an intention to cultivate gratitude, it can be easy to believe that despair, negativity, and hopelessness rule the day. News outlets and other media celebrate the downside, pointing out all there is to fear and feel angry about. Facilitators modeling appreciation and thankfulness for the good in the room and in the world help youth learn to cultivate this same attitude.

Don't ignore participants' grief to focus on gratitude (for example, responding to a teen grieving about her upcoming out-of-town move by telling her what she should be grateful for) or jump too quickly into gratitude when it might be useful to stay with more negative or hard-to-feel emotions. Don't pressure anyone who has trouble expressing gratitude, especially if he or she is having a challenging day. However, it is important to end all groups with a round of gratitude – no matter what has come up with the group.

Model honest, genuine behavior.

Be authentic and transparent without over-sharing or putting participants in a position in which they feel drawn to take care of the facilitator's needs instead of having their own needs met in the group.

Conversely, avoid under-sharing or withholding when having a challenging time. You don't need to force enthusiasm, stifle emotion or pretend that everything is OK. Sharing about the emotional state you are in without breaking down or getting into the deeper details of the reasons why sets a great example, especially when contradictory emotional states are present. It demonstrates the possibility of handling one's emotions well while being truthful and being open to empathy and support.

At check-in, facilitator Stefanie reports that she is sad that she has learned that her dog of 15 years is nearing the end of his life and needs to be put down. She wipes away a few tears. Participants are able to empathize, but they never have a sense that they need to take care of Stefanie; she is feeling her emotions, but not letting them take over her experience or the group's experience. Once she has shared this, she ends her check-in with a positive. "I'm feeling happy to be at group today. I appreciate everyone's listening and support."

Stefanie is doing an excellent job of sharing succinctly about a difficult issue in her life. She is modeling that it is possible to have two or more feelings at once; that it is okay to have sad feelings; and that these kinds of feelings can be safely shared in the group. If facilitators begin to withhold or over-share, participants quickly follow suit.

Prioritize integrity.

Integrity is the quality of being honest – of having strong moral principles and living in accordance with them. Integrity is "walking your talk." More broadly, integrity describes a state of being whole and undivided: of *being your word*. The AHA! Method offers adults a model for non-defensively, peacefully embodying their own beliefs. When facilitators model integrity, they build trust in the group.

Facilitators guide participants to live more in integrity when they create a safe space where all beliefs can be shared and lived by without fear of judgment or punishment. They lead group processes that help participants identify their own strong moral principles and to help them consider how they might live according to those principles. They give detailed positive reflections of the

34

ways in which youth are living in integrity and gently challenge out-of-integrity positions through questioning and discussion – all in a spirit of exploration rather than of imposing or condemning certain beliefs.

Exploration of integrity in the AHA! Method also involves guiding participants toward moral principles that do not involve harming, judging or holding prejudices against others; helping them learn to identify, communicate about and work through emotions that arise when others' integrity does not agree with their own; and continually reminding them that integrity is cultivated inside one's self and not determined by others.

During check-in, teen participant Ingrid says, "I can't believe it. My best friend just told me she's gay. I can't be her friend anymore. She might decide she's in love with me and then I'd have to beat her ass because I think that being gay is just wrong." Facilitator Gerard guides Ingrid to talk about her own experience of the situation. He asks her questions like, "What feelings come up for you when you think about your friend being gay?" With some questioning, he finds that she's sad and afraid to lose her best friend.

Gerard and his co-facilitators acknowledge that some people don't believe that homosexuality is OK, then guide Ingrid to discuss her fears and judgments with the group, her friend and others close to her in a non-violent, non-judging way. Ingrid learns skills for voicing her own beliefs about homosexuality without condemning anyone else. She is encouraged to make the choice about her friendship that fits with her beliefs as they are. If and when she decides to question those beliefs, she knows she has a safe place in which to do so.

Open up the conversation to opposing viewpoints to help others talk about their own beliefs in the same non-violent, non-judging manner. Ask them how they are living in integrity with their own beliefs. Create an activity in which each person talks about a belief he or she has that may be different from others, and what that's like. Model appreciation for the diversity of beliefs in the circle and the ability to discuss them without confrontation. Avoid imposing your own beliefs on participants or making their beliefs wrong. Follow up with curiosity, checking to see whether other participants want to contribute to the conversation.

This is not to say that facilitators should never feel conflicted or fragmented. We all do from time to time, especially when struggling to make difficult choices or having a bad day. Remaining in a place of integrity when these struggles emerge entails trusting the group process and being a whole-hearted participant in that process. Witnessing trusted mentors as they flow from a space lacking integrity into a new integral balance is another invaluable source of learning for participants.

Prioritize collaboration over competition.

A collaborative activity is one in which every participant feels a sense of cooperation with other participants. All input is valued. Guidelines are set by the group rather than by any one individual. It is non-adversarial, which maximizes the level of engagement by teens. This approach can be summed up with the phrase, "I want to win...and I want you to win, too."

A collaborative, win-win approach fosters social and emotional intelligence by creating an awareness of the experience of others. The collaborative approach also fosters self-confidence and strong social bonds, two qualities that are vital for successful navigation of the teen years. If the intention is to learn something new, it is most effective to do so in a calm, safe and non- competitive environment.

Facilitator Jess announces that today, the group is going to play the Counting Game, a simple activity that requires the group to work together to meet a goal. The clear goal is for the group to count and get as close to 10 without anyone speaking over anyone else. Getting to 10 on the first try is virtually impossible. As the group plays the game, participants call out a number at the same time in each round, which means the group has to start over. Jess' group struggles mightily. "We'll never reach 10!" says Javier. "Let's pick another number to aim for," Jess says, and they all agree that 7 is a reasonable goal. They soon get there. "Together, you set and reached a realistic goal, playing a difficult game," Jess says. "You all did it together by cooperating, listening and paying attention. Great work!" They talk about how it felt to work cooperatively and how having this experience has made them feel about themselves and each other.

Collaborative AHA! activities like the Counting Game bring a group together to accomplish a task. Sometimes this involves strategy; sometimes it involves physical work such as guiding people or objects through mazes or obstacle courses. The activity should be designed so that no one person has the information or ability to complete the task alone, and will be forced to rely on and trust others in the group. More cognitively based collaborative activities use the collective wisdom of the group to find solutions. Everyone's input is acknowledged and valued without negative judgment.

Any game or activity that divides the group into teams and emphasizes rewards for the winning team would be a competitive one. Competition mode stimulates "fight or flight" shifts in pulse and breathing, which may narrow focus and can stand in the way of exploring solutions. Under the pressure of competition, it can be easy to rest on what we think we know is right or best and to forget to empathize with others. Great mental energy and focus are required to remain open to everyone's input and values.

This being said: in AHA!, we do sometimes play games that involve winners and losers, because this gives us a chance to teach good sportsmanship – to focus on ways to be supportive and respectful whether we win or lose in a competitive situation. Competition brings fun and excitement to group activities, and can help facilitators experientially teach about the differing ways in which our bodies and minds respond to competition vs. collaboration.

The collaborative approach can be challenging for highly competitive individuals who are used to feeling a boost in self-esteem by winning and being right. This is an important point to acknowledge when it comes up in a group setting - that competitiveness can be addictive in its own way, and that choosing collaboration instead is a big and important step away from that mindset.

Prioritize collaborative approaches over directive approaches.

Working collaboratively with a group helps enroll them in both the process and the content of the day's activities. It gives participants a sense that they are not being "taught" or "led" but that they are cooperatively learning – from facilitators and each other.

To teach a segment about bullying, Daryanna and her co-facilitators allow a few minutes for each participant to share about their experiences with bullies.

Each facilitator shares as a participant him or herself. Only then does Daryanna take a few minutes to teach what she, as a facilitator, knows about the causes and impacts of bullying. At every step, she continues to enroll participants' input and participation so that they don't feel lectured to.

Frame activities as egalitarian and collaborative, rather than imposing them on the group. Use language that empowers participants. Maintain a strong leadership position, but make a frequent point of asking questions of participants that give them a sense of agency in the day's activities. Express appreciation for insights and ideas of participants. Be an equal participant in all group activities.

Challenges can arise when a collaborative approach takes more time than a directive approach in accomplishing tasks or resolving interpersonal conflict. Patience, creativity and a sense of humor all help to maintain the goal of collaboration.

Be curious about disturbing behavior and bigotry.

When a teen "acts out" – for example, by rolling his eyes when an adult is talking, making a demeaning comment towards an adult or other youth, calling someone a derogatory name, talking to a neighbor while someone else is sharing, or engaging in more serious rule-breaking that disrupts group activities – facilitators have a choice to make. How should we respond to this type of behavior?

The group is on a break. The youth are eating snacks and hanging out with each other and the staff. One of the teens starts dancing. Another teen laughs at him, saying, "You are so gay! You look like an idiot! You can't dance!" One of the staff members overhears this comment and approaches the teen with curiosity. "I overheard your comment. I'm wondering what you meant when you called Jack 'gay'?" This curiosity opens up a discussion about the power of words, what it means to be gay, and about participants' feelings about that topic.

A general attitude of curiosity is a constructive, self-preserving way to deal with negative or disturbing behaviors characteristic of teens. It allows you to be open, ask good questions, and support teens in coming around to more reasonable, positive actions and interactions of their own accord.

Many youth are raised with an authoritarian parenting style. They are expected to unconditionally follow strict rules that have been imposed upon them without explanation. Punishment or the threat of punishment, offset by little or no warmth or nurturing, may be used to enforce these rules. Youth parented in this way may come to associate obedience with love. They fail to develop self-discipline. Modeling their parents, they display more aggressive behavior towards others outside the home. They may act fearful or overly shy or lack self-esteem in social situations.

Some adults who work with youth may respond in an authoritarian, punitive manner in response to teens' acting-out, inflicting consequences and reprimanding the teen for his or her actions. Experience demonstrates that while this might work short-term to diminish the unwanted behavior, the teen is likely to go on the defensive and become unavailable to helpful input from facilitators. As the teen feels marginalized from the group, such behaviors will probably re-emerge.

When a facilitator approaches acting-out with an attitude of curiosity, youth feel acknowledged and are more likely to be open to change. A frank, non-judgmental conversation about the behavior allows the adult and other youth to learn from it. This increased understanding can lead to compassion, empathy, and establishment of a sense of personal responsibility.

Keep adult sharing minimal – only enough to provide stimulation and discussion.

Adults tend to over-share, lecture and monologue. This type of adult sharing is a barrier to complex teen brain development. The teen brain is constantly growing and creating new wiring, and interaction – not being talked at – is what they need to build their synapses. They need to respond, reflect, challenge, and struggle with concepts and ideas. Don't use teens as your captive audience because you need to be mirrored or like to perform.

Jess is teaching a component on the impact of marijuana on the brain. He lays out about five minutes of facts about memory, hormone impact, and throat irritation. He then has the teens divide into groups and make a list of the pros and cons of pot use, with consideration of social impact, family impact, academic costs and benefits, and health considerations. Jess then asks the teens to imagine a world where marijuana did not exist, and asks them to make a list of non-drug ways they could get the benefits equated with marijuana. This launches the class into a riveting discussion of the many obvious and subtle issues related to marijuana use.

The best adult facilitators know how to give just enough content to provide a stimulating launching point, and then ask key questions to further encourage great discussion and dialogue. This teaches, through example, how to share succinctly in an entire room of people who want to be heard.

Be friendly without being friends.

When working with teens, it is tempting to try to cultivate a buddy-like relationship. Some adults feel more comfortable when included in teens' tight cliques as a friend rather than outside of those cliques as an authority figure.

Teens do not need adults who act like their peers. They need adults who stand firm in their wisdom and maturity and maintain clear boundaries. At the same time, creating a culture of mutuality is more conducive to unfettered learning than a culture of "power-over" authority. Mutuality implies that qualities like respect, authenticity, transparency, accountability, and reliability are two-way streets. It fosters a climate where adults and teens are held to reciprocal standards.

When Stacy comes in late to a group, facilitator Jorge says to her, "Stacy, what held you up?" Stacy jokes, "Same thing that held you up last week, Jorge...I had something better to do."
"Stacy, I was late last week, and I shouldn't have been," Jorge replies. "I don't have anything better to do than keep my commitments. So. What held you up?"

This interaction demonstrates kindness without joining with Stacy's missteps as a teen. It also shows that adults are fallible and accountable for their mistakes.

Don't join in with the rebellious and immature acts of teens in order to appear cool in their eyes. If Stacy comes in late and Jorge says, "Hey, chica, you must have been having a good time to be this late," Jorge might receive a temporary moment of teen approval, but it will dilute his power to influence Stacy around issues of accountability. Jorge's behavior sends a message that being cool is more important than having integrity.

Where possible, have one facilitator who attends to content and another who attends to process.

In a group, content refers to what is being discussed: the subject at hand. Bullying, acceptance of others who may not be like us, dealing with emotions, or learning the value of service to others are examples of content we cover in AHA! groups.

Process refers to how content is being discussed. How are people saying what they are saying? What kind of nonverbal gestures and body language are evident? What's the subtext – the energy beneath the actual subject matter being addressed?

While content cannot be ignored and often needs to be guided, the process of a group can make the difference between a real experience of connection or an experience of participants staying at a surface level. Process and content are equally important, and it is easy to get carried away with content we are passionate about while forgetting to tend to process.

Allen comes to group and states the he wants to talk about poverty. He says it is a very serious problem for many people he knows. In a discussion round, each member says things like, "I agree," or "Yeah, poverty sucks." During the round, several of the youth look at the ceiling or their shoes; signal jokingly to one another; or otherwise appear to be checked out. Within three minutes, the group has covered the topic of poverty - at least, in terms of content. Clearly, the process has not gone very deep at all. Many of the youth seem to have more to say about this.

Kristen, the facilitator responsible for process, asks the group to do a second go-round. She asks each member to offer an example about how poverty has impacted him or her or someone they know, and to say a bit about how they feel about this. With this, she has moved to deepen the process of the group on the content of poverty.

Most of the interactions that teach social and emotional skills have more to do with process than content. In the AHA! Method, the importance of process is honored by assigning one leader to consciously focus on monitoring content while the other monitors process. This approach enables the group to stay on track with content while allowing process to help guide the day's activities.

Welcome participant feedback in developing content and process.

In order to remain relevant in a frantically changing world, programs that serve youth need to keep pace with shifts in youth culture and needs. Involve youth in critiquing the program and brainstorming new ideas for content delivery and group cohesion. Through written feedback or feedback loops, engage youth in looking back on previous sessions and telling you what they learned; what they would have liked to learn; what they didn't learn; and how the curriculum could be more alive for them. This doesn't mean you have to implement every idea, but youth will give you great grist for consideration. They are the experts on what really works for them. Soliciting their input will help them feel like stakeholders, which is good for everyone involved.

Ensure that facilitators de-brief as a group after sessions.

Part of the culture of AHA! is that as a community, we are always looking for opportunities to grow and learn from our activities and each other. We value feedback, observation, and insights that allow us to reflect on areas for growth and lend opportunities to appreciate personal and group strengths. In the debrief, we discuss what worked and what didn't work in that day's group activities, and we troubleshoot ways to improve in the future.

As the first day of the summer program winds to a close, all lingering teen participants are asked to leave the room so that the staff can debrief. They sit in a circle and one staff member is selected to lead. One facilitator answers, "I really felt we worked well as a team today. Each of us took responsibility to make sure that all teens felt included and supported. I want to say a special thank you to our group leader, Jane, who really held a strong center today." The next respondent shares, "I felt I showed up organized, prepared and present for today's activities, even though I have a lot going on in my personal life right now." Then, another debrief question is posed: "Please share how we could have improved the group today. Are there any changes you would like to see for next time?" A facilitator answers, "Today, when three staff members showed up late, I felt frustrated, because I didn't feel like I had the support I needed to get the group started. I really need to have all staff show up on time so that I can rely on their support." The circle closes with appreciations.

During this process, we each take responsibility for acknowledging areas for growth and for sharing how changes could enhance our personal success as well as the success of the program. In this way, we give and receive positive, constructive feedback in a supportive, loving, collaborative manner.

Recognize that change happens slowly.

Adolescents are in a process of extreme change and rapid brain development. Although they move quickly through things and seem to be ready for novelty at every second, they are slow to learn emotional and social lessons and values. Consistent, reliable mentorship over a period of years is required to support them in this learning.

Vanessa, a star group member for two years, has overcome almost every conceivable family obstacle - drugs, divorce, abuse, and a family without education — to become a stellar student and junior group leader. She is on track to graduate. In every way, she's exemplary. Then, one evening, she gets drunk and has sex with a guy in the back seat of a car. She ends up pregnant and chooses to keep the baby. Her plans for being the first member of her family to attend college are delayed. Although staff members of the youth organization that serves Vanessa are upset, they see it as an opportunity to keep mentoring her as she navigates this difficult transition. Years later, she stays in touch, and lets the organization know she's back on track to become who she wanted to be before her impulsive teen brain made one incalculably great mistake.

In some programs, participants are immersed in fast-working, intensely transformative processes that create huge front-end bangs and a temporary high. These "smash-and-grow" programs don't have lasting impact. They trickle steadily downwards after the initial high, and often create self-recrimination within teens that do not sustain the initial "wow" of the intensive workshop or seminar.

An approach that keeps youth involved over time acknowledges that real, lasting change takes time, and that it occurs in stages of learning and integration. Create a loose system of escalating responsibilities and benchmarks in your class or program to enable teens to continually aspire towards higher levels of effort, achievement and understanding.

Carla started our program as a 10th grader. By 12th grade, she had mastered much of the curriculum, but she still wanted to be challenged. We asked her to be an assistant to the adult leaders, and to be the ambassador to new youth and lonely youth. She felt proud to be the person assigned to make others welcome. With all the knowledge and compassion she had developed, she skillfully helped create the group culture.

Seemingly miraculous turnarounds should be regarded with caution. Facilitators whose expectations for assimilation and transformation are unrealistically high can set up a dynamic where teens feel pressured. They may not be able to get out of the group what they could if facilitators accepted that most youth need to go two steps forward and one or two steps backward to make lasting changes.

Understand and accept that no method works for every participant.

This method is strongly founded in mutuality, which necessitates mutual investment in process and outcomes. Some level of participant consent and engagement is necessary. When someone really does not want to participate, the overall exuberance and vitality of the group is reduced. A student/participant who honestly states, "I don't want to be here, but I have to," and who is not just in a bad mood but truly does not want to be there at all, will have a counterproductive impact on every other participant in the room.

Active substance abusers that come altered to classes or groups won't gain much from the program, and their presence will detract from the experience of peers who show up sober and committed. Youth in need of intensive therapeutic care due to developmental or emotional disabilities should be carefully assessed. They should only participate if they can do so without straining facilitators to such a degree that the rest of the group suffers. If Joey consistently breaks down sobbing or acts out disruptively in some other way, it may be too difficult to attend to Joey's extra needs and run the method.

When any one member requires too much individual attention to enable facilitators to effectively run the group, it is best to refer that member to a more structured environment where he or she can get more personalized attention.

Where a student has negative feedback about the program, facilitators should hear it without reacting defensively or angrily, setting the stage for the possibility of these kinds of responses for participants in their own lives. It demonstrates to participants that their input is valuable and that there is a time and place for it to be brought up and discussed. Allowing a student to walk away when the program is definitely not working for him or her shows the group that it's okay to walk away from something that doesn't work for you, and that there's a kind, non-violent way to say no to something you don't want.

Part Two

Emotional Intelligence

EQ: An Introduction

Emotional intelligence is the ability to recognize feelings in one's self and to understand and manage them. Inherent in this is the ability to delay action or gratification and to recognize the link between thoughts and feelings. EQ refers to Emotional Quotient, which is a person's mastery level of emotional skills. If you have high EQ, it means you are good with people. You listen well and are compassionate. You connect with others easily and satisfy your own needs cooperatively. Research demonstrates that children with high EQ are more confident, learn better, have fewer behavior problems, and are more optimistic and happy.

Emotional intelligence describes abilities to:

- Express emotions appropriately
- Manage challenging emotions
- Regulate our own emotions
- Problem-solve and evaluate risk, using information yielded by emotions
- Resolve conflicts where emotions run high
- Recognize, sensitively inquire about, and empathize with the emotions of others
- Delay gratification

Emotions are important for survival, decision-making, boundary setting, communication, unity and empathy. Teens can easily misinterpret or act on their emotions in ways that work against their own best interests and the interests of their families and communities. Taking the time to teach them how to be emotionally intelligent and to hear/heed messages from their bodies is an important way of supporting their achievement, success and happiness.

- **Emotions and survival:** Our emotions evolved over millions of years, resulting with the potential to serve as a delicate yet sophisticated internal guidance system. Emotions alert us when natural human needs are not being met: when we feel lonely, our need for connection with other people is unmet; when we feel afraid, our need for safety is unmet; and when we feel rejected, our need for acceptance is unmet.

- **Emotions and decision-making:** Our emotions are a valuable source of information that helps us make decisions. Studies show that when certain neural pathways related to emotion are severed in the brain, the simplest decisions become impossible to make.

- **Emotions and body intelligence:** Body intelligence is the ability to listen to and discern the body's physical cues – to hear its intuitive messages and find the courage to trust them. It goes hand-in-hand with emotional intelligence, creating an inner wisdom that helps individuals establish clear personal boundaries, develop a respectful relationship with their bodies, and create strategies for self-management based on information they receive from their own mental and physical selves. Many emotions are announced to our awareness through "body clues" – sensations that come up in the body when we have a certain feeling. When you are angry, does the back of your neck start to feel hot and prickly, or does your lip start to twitch? When you are sad, do you feel a hollowing in the pit of your stomach or constriction in your chest? These are body clues. Trusting one's gut means attending to these kinds of clues. Most people, when asked to identify where they feel an emotion in their bodies, struggle to identify or describe those sensations.

- **Boundary setting:** When we feel uncomfortable with another person's behavior, our emotions alert us. If we learn to trust our emotions and feel confident in expressing them, we can responsibly relay or act upon our feelings of discomfort as soon as we're aware of them. We may simply ask to be heard, make a request, or enter into discussion. This helps us to set personal boundaries necessary to protect our physical and emotional health.

- **Emotions and communication:** Our emotions help us communicate with others. Our facial expressions, for example, can convey a wide range of emotions. If we look sad or hurt, we are signaling to others that something is wrong. We may be signaling the need for support or distance, depending on how we handle these emotions. If we're verbally skilled, we will be able to express more of our emotional needs and will have a better chance of meeting them. If we are effective at listening to the emotional challenges of others, we are better able to help them feel understood, valued and cared for.

- **Unity:** Emotions are universal for human beings. Among humans, the emotions of empathy, compassion, cooperation, and forgiveness are commonly shared. Beliefs can divide us; healthy emotions coupled with empathy can bring us all closer.

- **Empathy:** Empathy allows us to identify with another's feelings; to emotionally put ourselves in another's place. It can lead us to treat others in more compassionate ways. The ability to empathize is directly dependent on our ability to feel our own feelings and identify them. Those who have deeply experienced the widest range of feelings are able to empathize with the greatest diversity of people from all corners of the earth. When we say that someone "can't relate" to other people, it is likely because they haven't experienced, acknowledged or accepted many feelings of their own. Our own experiences of feeling states give us the emotional vocabulary we need to recognize and respond appropriately to similar emotional responses in others. Empathy is only possible for those who are open to experiencing their own emotions – who do not distract themselves from them or numb themselves with drugs or alcohol. Awareness of what we are feeling leads to the ability to acknowledge, identify and accept our feelings, and then to empathize with others.

Ways to Build and Express Emotional Intelligence

Here are some guidelines for making EQ an integral part of your work with youth.

Use feeling words.

An extensive vocabulary of feeling words helps facilitators and students to accurately name and describe their emotions. Here are a few to begin with. Add to the list as you see fit, and invite participants to do the same.

HAPPY: Cheerful, Delighted, Ecstatic, Elated, Festive, Fortunate, Glad, Gleeful, Important, Joyous, Jubilant, Lucky, Merry, Overjoyed, Satisfied, Sunny, Thankful

ALIVE: Animated, Courageous, Energetic, Free, Frisky, Impulsive, Liberated, Optimistic, Playful, Provocative, Spirited, Thrilled, Wonderful

GOOD: At ease, Blessed, Bright, Calm, Certain, Clever, Comfortable, Content, Encouraged, Free and easy, Peaceful, Pleased, Quiet, Reassured, Relaxed, Serene, Surprised

INTERESTED: Absorbed, Affected, Concerned, Curious, Engrossed, Fascinated, Inquisitive, Intrigued, Nosy, Snoopy

POSITIVE: Eager, Keen, Earnest, Intent, Anxious, Inspired, Determined, Excited, Enthusiastic, Bold, Brave, Daring, Challenged, Optimistic, Confident, Hopeful

LOVING: Admiring, Affectionate, Attracted, Close, Comforting, Considerate, Devoted, Drawn toward, Loved, Passionate, Sensitive, Sympathetic, Tender, Touched, Warm

ANGRY: Aggressive, Annoyed, Bitter, Cross, Enraged, Hateful, Hostile, Incensed, Indignant, Inflamed, Infuriated, Insulting, Irritated, Offensive, Provoked, Resentful, Sore, Unpleasant, Upset, Worked up

AFRAID: Alarmed, Anxious, Cowardly, Doubtful, Fearful, Frightened, Menaced, Nervous, Panicky, Quaking, Restless, Scared, Shaky, Suspicious, Terrified, Threatened, Timid, Wary, Worried

CONFUSED: Disillusioned, Distrustful, Doubtful, Hesitant, Indecisive, Lost, Misgiving, Perplexed, Pessimistic, Shy, Skeptical, Stupefied, Tense, Unbelieving, Uncertain, Uneasy, Unsure, Upset

HELPLESS: Alone, Despairing, Distressed, Dominated, Empty, Fatigued, Forced, Frustrated, Hesitant, Incapable, Inferior, Paralyzed, Pathetic, Tragic, Useless, Vulnerable, Woeful

DEPRESSED: A sense of loss, Abominable, Ashamed, Bad, Despicable, Detestable, Disappointed, Discouraged, Dissatisfied, Guilty, In despair, Lousy, Miserable, Powerless, Repugnant, Sulky

HURT: Aching, Afflicted, Agonized, Alienated, Appalled, Crushed, Dejected, Deprived, Heartbroken, Humiliated, Injured, Offended, Pained, Rejected, Tormented, Tortured, Victimized, Wronged

SAD: Anguished, Desolate, Desperate, Dismayed, Grieving, Lonely, Mournful, Pained, Pessimistic, Sorrowful, Tearful, Unhappy

DISGUSTED: Revulsion, Loathing, Abhorrence, Distaste

ASHAMED: Apologetic, Contrite, Guilty, Regretful, Remorseful Repentant, Rueful, Sheepish

EMBARRASSED: Agitation, Awkwardness, Blushing, Humiliation, Self-consciousness, Sheepishness, Tongue-tied, Upset

Adapted from www.psychpage.com:
http://www.psychpage.com/learning/library/assess/feelings.html

Differentiate between thoughts and feelings.

Differentiating between thoughts and feelings creates clearer communication and helps avoid statements that could be perceived as blaming or judgmental. It's common for people to use the word "feel" when they are actually describing a thought, and this can mean we are blaming or projecting expectations on ourselves or others.

In general, we are expressing a thought and not a feeling when the word feel is followed by:

The words "that," "like," or "as if"
"I feel that you should know better."
"I feel like a failure."
"I feel as if I am living with a wall."

The pronouns I, you, he, she, they, it
"I feel I am always wrong."
"I feel it is useless."
"I feel they are making fun of me."

Names or nouns referring to people
"I feel Amy has been pretty responsible."
"I feel my teacher is manipulative."

These are statements of judgment/thought, not of true feeling states.

To avoid conflating feelings and thoughts or needs, distinguish between how a person feels and what that person thinks about others' reaction or behavior towards them. "I feel unimportant to the people I go to school with." Unimportant describes how I think others are evaluating me. "I'm discouraged and/or sad" would better describe the actual feeling.

"I feel misunderstood." Here, misunderstood indicates my assessment of the other person's level of understanding. I may be feeling anxious or annoyed.

"I feel ignored." This is an interpretation of the actions of others rather than a clear statement of how I am feeling. We may be feeling hurt because we are being left out. Ignored is an example of a word we may use to interpret others rather than express how we feel.

While it can seem overly picky to make this distinction, it can help us to drop from a story about how others are treating or regarding us into an actual experience of our own emotional states (thereby increasing our EQ).

Make physical sensations related to feelings part of the conversation.

Sensations are the actual somatic or physical experiences that occur in our bodies. Expressing body sensations is a helpful way to touch into feelings. Check in with students about how their bodies feel. Is there tension? Where is it situated? Or is there pain, or butterflies, or numbness?

"I notice a feeling of jumpiness in my stomach."
"There is a shudder in the back of my neck."

"My body feels light."

"I feel breathless."

Descriptions like these lead participants to a better awareness of their feeling states, and allows them to experience those states fully rather than acting them out in potentially destructive ways:

Achy	Airy	Bloated
Blocked	Breathless	Bubbly
Buzzy	Chills	Clammy
Cold	Congested	Constricting
Cool	Damp	Dense
Dizzy	Dull	Electric
Energized	Expanding	Faint
Flowing	Fluid	Flushed
Fluttery	Frantic	Frozen
Fuzzy	Goose-bumpy	Hot
Intense	Itchy	Jagged
Jittery	Jumpy	Light
Limp	Mild	Moist
Nauseous	Numb	Paralyzed
Pressure	Prickly	Pulsing
Quaking	Quivery	Radiating
Shaky	Sharp	Shivery
Shudder	Smooth	Spinning
Stringy	Suffocating	Sweaty
Tense	Thick	Tight
Tingly	Twitchy	Vibration
Welling-up	Wobbly	Withering

Emotional Flooding

One important reason to teach EQ to teens is to help them understand and react constructively to what's known as emotional flooding. Emotional flooding is a state of being so overwhelmed by feeling that we literally cannot think straight.

Emotional flooding is the result of an interaction between parts of the brain known as the cerebral cortex and the amygdalae:

- The amygdalae, two almond-shaped glands perched above either side of the brainstem, are responsible for activating emotional centers and stimulating the fight-or-flight response. There, emotionally potent events are remembered, and they inspire scanning for events that resemble them – an effort to self-preserve by protecting against traumatic
- influences.
- The cerebral cortex is the largest and most recently evolved portion of the brain. It receives sensory information, coordinates sensory and motor activities, and is the seat of higher cognitive processes. When an environmental stimulus is strong enough, it may bypass the cortex and go directly to the amygdala. This stimulates the adrenal glands (atop the kidneys) to release hormones (adrenaline), causing heart rate and blood pressure to increase and muscles to prepare for quick action.
- This process happens before the cortical centers know what's happening. There is little or no cognitive perspective. The thinking brain is effectively disconnected from the feeling, reactive brain. This leaves the body in survival mode

and creates a "fight, flight, or freeze" response.

When the heart rate escalates to over 100 beats per minute, the person is considered to be flooded or "emotionally hijacked," and no longer has the ability to utilize cognitive thought enough to negotiate or communicate rationally. At least 20 minutes will need to pass before the fight/flight/freeze hormones are metabolized. This means that once the flood occurs, a 20-minute calm-down period is required for the cortex to re-connect.

Sometimes, the emotional flooding response is triggered not based on what happens now, but in perceptions or memories that may have formed years ago, even during infancy. We react in an old way to a new situation. Intense fight-or-flight responses that arise in these moments may involve extreme rage or fear.

Learning this information and how to apply it is one of the best reasons to use the AHA! Method in teen classrooms – places full of people in a developmental stage where this kind of flooding is common. It helps those who work with teens to better understand behaviors that seem, at their surface, outrageous.

Teaching Teens About Emotional Flooding

AHA! uses simplified language to explain these concepts to youth:

- The limbic system and amygdala are the "old brain" (fight, flight, freeze).
- The cerebral cortex is the "new brain" (logic, consequences, higher thinking).
- The old brain reacts to big emotions via the fight-or-flight

system, triggering release of a flood of adrenaline into the bloodstream.

- This flood effectively cuts off access to the new brain, shutting down any possibility of applying higher thought to the situation.

- It is in this state that we're likely to make choices we will regret later.

- By learning to recognize "body clues" – heart racing, feeling hot, sweating, hands feeling like they want to punch or push something, lip twitching, or even a sense of numbness – that begin to show up *before* adrenaline is released, they can learn to stop themselves from continuing in a situation where this is likely to happen: "I can feel my lip twitching/heart racing/body starting to heat up, and I know if I keep going right now I will probably say or do something I'll regret. Let me go take a few minutes to cool down and we can come back to this."

- It takes at least 20 minutes for this adrenaline flood to wear off enough for us to re-connect to the new brain.

AHA! uses experiential activities and small and large group discussion to guide youth in exploring their own body clues and talking about ways to defuse, calm down, and engage in self-care when flooded.

A Toolbox for Coping with Emotional Flooding

EQ tools are designed, in part, to promote effectiveness in coping with emotional flooding. These tools include:

Mindfulness: to deliberately observe present experience without interfering with it.

Witnessing: the witness is the "meta-observer" – the part of us that can observe or notice our experience. Witnessing is being able to describe, discuss and understand our feeling states rather than acting on them.

Focusing: in this context, the ability to focus on what is happening in our minds and bodies, mindfully, without reacting to or attaching to any one thing.

Owning our projections: Projections generally occur when we have a judgment or opinion about someone else, when the issue is really about something that needs to be healed inside of ourselves. The stronger the reaction to the other person, the more likely it is that we are projecting. Particularly, when we feel oppressed, the usual reaction is to point a finger at or blame another for the pain that we experience. This, too, is a signal that we are projecting onto someone else rather than looking inward at what we might need to heal or shift.

Supporting teens in owning their projections leads them to better understand themselves and their emotions. They become less prone to flooding, blaming, and harming others when they are feeling bad. They develop the ability to look inward for comfort and to use irritation at others as a way to better understand themselves. The same is true for facilitators. Consider, when you feel emotionally flooded around something someone else is doing, whether it is pointing to something you need to be working on in yourself.

As youth develop the ability to feel the coming flood and to take steps to curtail it, they can begin to choose to proactively move through the intensity and solve whatever issue is creating the threat of flooding. In the box below, find some additional action steps that can help youth feel more capable in managing tough emotions. Try creating a role-playing game or other activity where youth explore these options in test scenarios.

25 Ways to Deal With Difficult Moments, Situations, or Feelings

When uncomfortable or unpleasant emotions arise, try one or more of these suggestions to access a more comfortable emotional state, or to head off an emotional flood without fighting against or repressing feelings.

1. **Name it to tame it.** Identify, as clearly as you can, what you are feeling.
2. **Meditate.** This can be as simple as sitting still and breathing with eyes closed for a few minutes. Try paying attention to the sensation of air entering and leaving through the nose. This technique serves to "cool" the mind between two difficult meetings or during transitions in the day – for example, the transition between work and home.
3. **Seek another ear.** Call a friend or trusted family member. Ask if he or she can lend you their ears for a few minutes, then express what comes to your mind.
4. **Turn yourself off.** Rest or sleep a little. Sometimes change happens when we simply tune out, leaving thoughts and feelings to process themselves as we rest.
5. **Brainstorm.** Grab paper and a pen and write everything…everything that comes to your mind. Then, throw it away.
6. **Get moving!** Take a walk, run, swim, dance, or practice a sport.
7. **Wait 'til it passes.** Just do nothing. Wait at least twenty minutes before taking any action.

8. **Pay attention to the present.** Direct your attention to the space around you for a few minutes. Notice the colors, shapes, sounds, and textures of your immediate environment.

9. **Awaken the witness.** Notice the part of you that is able to observe your actions, thoughts, and reactions. Ask yourself: What am I thinking about? What am I imagining? Am I repeating a certain behavior? You might notice that part of what's making you upset is that you are hearing an internal voice telling you that you did something wrong. Another possibility is that we may be reacting to an imagined, projected future.

10. **Check in with body sensations.** Notice sensations: their location, intensity, and movement within.

11. **Do something enjoyable.** What's your pleasure? A hot bath, a sauna, enjoying a sunset or the stars, the feel or smell of a flower? Feel as much pleasure as you can. Immerse yourself in it thoroughly for at least a few minutes.

12. **Adjust your expectations.** A person with overblown expectations of stability can feel bad just because her natural state variation doesn't mesh with her unrealistic expectation. Expectations that life should be like a straight line reduce our tolerance for the peaks, valleys, curves and angles that typically make up our days.

13. **Believe and imagine.** Sometimes we don't take action to solve a particular issue because we don't believe that it's possible to find a solution. To deal with this, try for some moments to act as if it is possible, just to direct your mind to a way through the problem at hand. You already know how to do this. If asked, "What would you do if you were the President?" or "What would it be like for you to travel to

Japan?" you could a generate fantasy of what is possible.

14. **Smile or laugh.** Watch a funny movie, read a book of jokes, or do something else that brings out your light side. Laughter alters neurochemistry in positive ways and is generally conducive to good health.

15. **Interpret it better.** Imagine that the apparently negative event you're experiencing has a positive potential. For example, if you are delayed by traffic or stuck at an airport, think of all the ways slowing down and taking downtime could be beneficial. You could read a newspaper, listen to the news and become more informed, or listen to soothing music and reflect upon your life.

16. **"Chunk down."** Decide what to do just for the next minute, or less. Try resolving one aspect of a single issue – "chunking down" – or, at least, taking a baby step towards it.

17. **Work with your breath.** Direct your attention to your breathing. Gradually allow it to slow, letting your abdomen expand with each inhalation and gently fall with each exhalation.

18. **Be of service.** Focusing on someone else's needs for a short time can bring needed perspective to your own problems. Do something thoughtful and generous that requires effort and removes you from your usual routine.

19. **Relax your posture.** Loosen your brow. Loosen your other muscles, too. Scan the body internally, looking for pockets of tension. Let your attention linger there as this tension ebbs out. Try starting with an arm, a hand, even a finger, and then work your way into broader areas of the body. Or change how you feel by changing your body posture in other ways: assume the posture of a saint...an action hero...or a comedian.

20. **Read a good book and/or watch a good film.** Within reason, escapism can be soothing and relaxing. Removing yourself from engagement with others can help release stress.

21. **Apply your experience or someone else's strategy.** Search in your memory for a similar situation that was solved by you, then apply a similar strategy. Or, if you know someone who's already solved a similar matter, do what he or she has done.

22. **Work with a metaphor.** We've all related to metaphors since childhood. Using a metaphor to describe your emotions can be a form of guided meditation that you can then use to change your inner state. If your emotion were a lake or a volcano, what characteristics would it have? If it's erupting, imagine it calming and growing peaceful. If it's a rough sea, imagine its waves becoming less turbulent and its surface becoming smooth as glass.

23. **Change your environment.** Many times we create "anchors" or associations to specific events. These anchored responses to the environment can be re-stimulated when we see a particular image or hear a specific sound – as happens when a couple hears "their song," which brings up feelings of love or nostalgia. Negative associations to certain environments can trigger emotional flooding.

24. **Practice gratitude.** Think of three things you've been grateful for. Even if they are small things or things you have often taken for granted, an attitude of gratitude can shift your perspective dramatically.

25. **In accordance with your beliefs, ask the universe for help.** Allow yourself to have an attitude of openness, receptivity, permission to receive and acceptance of the help.

Some of the above comes from the work of Virgílio Vasconcelos Vilela. Thanks to Evely Garcia, from São Paulo, for comments and suggestions. Copyright 2001-2002 Virgílio Vasconcelos Vilela. Reproduction authorized if author and source mentioned; please acknowledge.

Part Three

The AHA! Method in Action

The AHA! Group: Overview

With the foundational pieces of group facilitation and emotional intelligence in place, you are ready to move into the more practical aspects of the AHA! Method.

The basic elements of an AHA! group meeting are listed below, with more detailed explanations following later in this chapter:

Thorns and Roses or other check-in. A chance for all participants to check in with a brief share about how their days are going. Briefer check-ins can also be used with larger groups or where time is tight.

Follow-ups. Where time allows, youth are given a few minutes following check-in to ask one another follow-up questions.

Mindfulness. We lead youth in a brief mindfulness meditation; as time passes, youth can be asked to lead mindfulness segments.

Warm-Up or game. The AHA! Method relies on active team-building, creative, or teaching games to create group connectedness through play. Several games are described in this section of the manual.

Break. A snack break gives youth time to connect outside of the structure of the group.

Main activity. This usually includes a brief instructional or guiding segment or instructions, followed by discussion or other activities in the large group or in small groups. Often, the main activity will involve Council circle or Connection Circles.

Gratitude/Take-away. AHA! groups nearly always close with either a round of gratitude, where each person states one thing for which he or she is grateful; or a "take-away" – something he or she has learned or gained from that day's group.

Debrief. Make sure members of the group have a chance to share with each other about the experience. Debriefing may also happen after check-in or warm-ups/games.

Closing. In the large group, find a way to close on a positive, nourishing note.

If you are an out-of-school program, you may be able to follow this format fairly closely, designing your main activity around whatever your program wishes to emphasize. If you work in a school and have academic curriculum to teach, this curriculum would be at the heart of your main activity.

Enhancing Social-Emotional Intelligence

As you move through an AHA! group session, always be on the lookout for opportunities to teach social-emotional learning concepts. Look for ways to acknowledge and discuss participants' experiences of the six domains of social-emotional learning:

Emotional management – Ability to be aware of and constructively handle both positive and challenging emotions

Empathy – Relating to others with acceptance, understanding, and sensitivity to their diverse perspectives and experiences

Teamwork – Abilities to collaborate and coordinate with others.

Responsibility – Dispositions and abilities to reliably meet commitments and fulfill obligations of challenging roles

Initiative – Capacities to take action, sustain motivation, and persevere through challenge toward an identified goal

Problem Solving – Abilities to plan, strategize, and implement complex tasks

This can happen in the context of an activity, but be wary of interfering with an activity's momentum by introducing more didactic content. Usually it works best to bring out these concepts in a debrief following an activity or at the end of a group session.

The above domains are sourced from the Preparing Youth to Thrive Initiative: Smith C., McGovern G, Larson R, Hillaker B, Peck SC (2016). *Preparing Youth to Thrive: Promising Practices for Social Emotional Learning.* Forum for Youth Investment, Washington, D.C.

Check-In

We begin all AHA! groups with a check-in, which serves several functions:

- To create a sense of community
- To build empathy
- To gather information
- To create awareness of the mood of the group and its individual members
- As a basic warm-up or icebreaker

The objective at the start of all AHA! sessions is to unite the group by establishing a common theme or focus. This focus or theme is often established during the check-in, where each group member has a chance to share with the rest of the group.

Check-in is generally conducted seated in a circle. Moving clockwise, each person speaks without interruption or cross-talk. A talking piece can be used, or each speaker can "fist bump" or otherwise make physical contact with the next person to pass check-in along.

With Thorns and Roses, each person begins with his or her name, then shares a "thorn" (something not going well or presenting a challenge) and a rose (something going well or for which one is grateful). This can be about what's going on today, this week, or in a broader sense.

As a facilitator, your approach at the start of any session sets the tone for the entire group. Before starting an AHA! session, take a moment to check in with your own emotions. Notice whether you are sad, angry, tired, joyful or fearful. Don't try to change your emotional state; just try to incorporate a statement about how you are doing at the start of the session, during check-in.
For example, a facilitator who feels exhausted might say: "My thorn is I'm really tired today, and my rose is I'm glad to be here and look forward to feeling more energized."

Number Check-In. Each participant checks in with a number from zero (a very challenging day) to 10 (best day ever).

Weather Report. The Weather Report is a non-threatening method of check-in that does not require participants to be specific. It enables them to inform the group about how they're doing, using terms that refer to the weather. Someone who is angry or frustrated and has a problem that seems unresolvable might say that his weather is stormy, with no sign of clearing. Another participant who feels good might describe sunny skies. Fogginess may be used to describe a feeling of being dulled, sleepy or confused. Once participants get the hang of this, creativity abounds.

Emotions Check-In. Each participant states three emotions he or she has felt today, or an emotion he or she feels right now.

Other creative avenues for check-in might be to pose questions like, "If you were a shoe right now, what kind of shoe would you be?" or "Considering how you feel right now, what kind of animal would best describe you?" These playful questions brilliantly wake up the group and get the laughter going.

Mindfulness

The AHA! Method also usually includes a brief mindfulness segment at some point in the session. Educational research finds that mindfulness is incredibly supportive for emotional management, which in turn is helpful for youth in both their academic and relationship lives.

A simple few minutes of stillness in meditation, focusing on the breath, is a great start. Consult any of the wonderful books or Web sites on mindfulness practices for more ideas.

Keep in mind that youth who have suffered trauma or are experiencing anxiety or depression may struggle with mindfulness practices. Give them options like keeping their eyes open while meditating or with doing a slow walking meditation instead of staying seated. Always normalize that some people dislike or feel uncomfortable within any mindfulness activity.

Warm-Ups and Games

These warm-ups and games can be used as icebreakers or blending activities, to start a group session, to bring people closer using play, or to wake up a group when a session bogs down or loses focus. They are derived from theater games and movement games that wake up the body, invigorate group interaction and help to establish or re-establish focus and concentration.

When facilitating games and warm-ups:

- Try always to be a participant rather than an observer.
- Be enthusiastic!
- Give clear, concise direction.
- Move through games quickly, keeping it upbeat and silly.
- Don't give participants a chance to second-guess or become insecure.
- Make note of positive choices and accomplishments in the context of these games; acknowledge them to participants

with energy and enthusiasm.

Choose games that dovetail well with participant energy during check-in. If the group seems low or sad, choose exercises to boost energy; if youth are overly energetic and scattered, choose exercises that will bring focus and calm.

Energizing Games

These physical games get the energy moving and help youth connect in fun ways.

Shake It Out!

Vigorously shake out one hand, then the other; then one foot, and then the other. With each limb, count out with gusto from 1-8, then 1-7, then 1-6, and so on, until you're shaking each limb only once.

Hours of the Day

Participants act out what they do on a typical day. The facilitator directs them to assume the physical posture they have at 6 am, then 7 am, and so on through the entire day, all the way back through to 6 am. A good one for getting participants involved in a gentle, fun way.

High Fives

Have participants quickly perform two-handed high-fives with as many other participants as possible in 30 seconds. "You have 30 seconds...GO!"

Mirroring

In pairs, one partner enacts motions and facial expressions. The other partner mirrors what the first partner does. Give each partner two to three minutes before switching. Afterwards, ask: What made it difficult to lead or follow? Did the leader make it easy for you to follow? How are the ways you lead and follow in this exercise like the ways you lead and follow in your life?

Hand-To-Hand, Back-To-Back

Facing each other, partners join open hand to open hand, pushing as hard as they can. Repeat just this part 10 times. Then, direct the partners to see how far they can move their feet away from each other while still pushing with their open hands, creating a triangle of cooperation.

Ask participants to switch partners and then to push with open hands with 2-3 others in the group.

Or…Have two participants stand back to back and push against each other as hard as they can. Direct them to sit down while still pushing and to then use the same force to stand up.

Blending Games

These games help participants get to know one another, feel connected, and have fun together while collaborating and cooperating. They support youth in "de-magnetizing" – connecting with youth outside their usual peer group.

Have You Ever?

Have participants stand in a circle with one volunteer in the center. The person in the center first states his or her name: "Hi, my name is _____," and the group responds: "Hi, _____!"

The center person then asks a question starting with "Have you ever…" and finishes the question by naming something he or she has done.

Everyone in the circle that would answer "Yes" to this question has to stand. Every person who is standing then moves to a new spot in the circle.

Switching places with the person next to you is against the rules. The last person left in the middle goes back into the center to start the next round.

Line-Ups

Facilitator has group line up shoulder-to-shoulder, facing one side of the room.

The facilitator announces that this is a silent activity. Then, he or she has the group create a line – without talking – with one or more of the following guidelines:

- Tallest to shortest
- Color of eyes: darkest to lightest
- Number of siblings in household: most to least
- Oldest to youngest (month, day, year)
- Luckiest to unluckiest
- Physically strongest to weakest
- Emotionally strongest to weakest
- Expresses emotion more or less easily
- Most to least adventurous
- Most to least risk-taking
- Messiest to cleanest
- Most emotional to least emotional
- Level of respect: most to least (toward parents, police, homeless, one's self)

After certain line-ups, facilitators can ask questions about why particular people are at one end or the other. Always end with positivity or playfulness.

People to People

People to People is a great way to de-magnetize youth and to foster connection in the group. The facilitator begins by having the group stand in a circle. This circle marks the boundary that cannot be crossed during this game. The participants must stay on the inside of this circle. The facilitator will ask the group to "mingle" (walk around). Participants can be asked to do this silently, while making eye contact with others as they pass, or they can be asked to do this in silly ways to break the ice (mingle around as monkeys, mingle around making the most awkward eye contact that you can). The facilitator will then yell out a direction – for example, "elbow to elbow" or "toe to toe." The participants must find the person closest to them and connect with their elbows, toes, or whatever the leader says. If participants don't feel comfortable with the touch, that is okay!

Once each group member finds a person with whom to connect, the leader will say, "Introduce yourself to your partner and answer the following question..." Facilitators may ask any questions with varying depth as they see fit. Once the pairs have enough time to answer, the facilitator asks for several shout-outs where participants can share their own answer. It's best not to have folks share their partner's answers without their permission.

Have the group mingle and connect using different body parts for several rounds of questions. Be sure to feel the vibe of the room. It is always best to end when there is still some energy in the game.

Don't wait for it to die to stop.

Facilitators can also call out numbers instead of "elbow to elbow" or "knee to knee." If the facilitator calls out "three," then participants must get into groups of three. Once they are in their groups of 3 the facilitator can ask a question like, "Find three things everyone in your pod has in common," or "If your pod received twenty dollars, what would you all do with it together?" Be sure that no matter the variation, youth should de-magnetize and connect with different people every round.

Three Name Games

- *Name Game With a Gesture:* Everyone stands in a circle. Each participant says his/her name along with a gesture. The whole group repeats the name along with the gesture. Repeat for each group member. You can add a noise to the gesture for a second round.

- *Name Game With an Adjective:* Have everyone stand or sit in a circle. Someone volunteers to begin and says his/her name plus an adjective that starts with the same letter as the name: "Jolly Janet," "Hungry Henry," "Vivacious Violet." The person next in the circle must say the person's name and adjective, then share his/her own name and adjective. Each person has more adjectives/names to remember than the one before. The last person must say each person's name and adjective along with his or her own.

- *Name Game With Shaking Hands:* The leader gives the group 30 seconds to shake hands and exchange names with at least five people. Participants must continuously shake hands until they have clasped hands with the next person, at which point they can release the first person's hand. After the initial 30 seconds, the leader gives another 30 seconds; this time, participants must shake hands and exchange names with different people than in the first round.

Speed Dating

Have the group sit in a circle.

Have everyone pair off with the person to his or her left, turning his or her chair so it faces that person's chair. The result will be an inner circle facing out and an outer circle facing in, with each group member partnered with another group member.

Participants in the outer circle will be "A" and in the inner circle "B."

The facilitator explains: "I'm going to read a list of questions. For each question, each partner will have one minute to answer, then we'll swap to the next partner."

Facilitator reads out the first question, then announces who will go first (A or B) in answering the question. After a minute, he or she announces the switch to the other person, who then answers the same question.

Once both partners have answered the question, the facilitator has people in the A group get up and move one person over to the left to talk with a new partner.

A new question is asked, and the facilitator can announce that the other letter goes first this time. The rotation can continue until the A's are back to the partner with whom they started the round.

Speed Dating Questions

Easy

- Do you like cats or dogs? Why?
- If you could be invisible, where would you go?
- What is your favorite movie? Why?
- What do you like to do in your free time/on weekends?
- If you could be an animal, which one would you be, and why?
- If you could have any superpower, what would it be?
- Where would you like to travel and why? What hobby do you love the most?
- What does your ideal day look like?
- If you could have dinner with three people, alive or dead, fictional or non-fictional, who would they be?
- If a natural disaster occurred, what three things would you grab from your house?
- What is your favorite food?
- If you could pick a color/animal/ice cream/food that represents you, what would it be and why?
- If you were stranded on an island, what five things, people, or foods would you bring, and why?

More Challenging

- Who do you live with? Who do you get along with best?
- What are your future goals?

- What's the nicest thing someone has done for you? What's the nicest thing you've done for someone else?
- What most/least excites you about high school?
- If you could be somebody else, who would you be and why?
- Three things you're really good at?
- Three wishes?
- Hopes for the next 5-10 years?
- Goals for the future?
- Name three things you want to do before you die.
- If you had a month to live, what would you do?
- If you could change one thing about the world, realistic or not, what would it be?
- What qualities do leaders have? Which of these qualities do you possess? Which do you need to work on?

Difficult

- What do you love/find challenging about your family?
- What will you do the same/differently than your parents when raising your own children?
- What is your fondest/worst childhood memory?
- What are you most proud of?
- If you could change something about yourself, what would it be and why?
- What do you appreciate/like about yourself most?
- If you could change one thing about yourself or your family history, what would it be?
- Who would your parents/family consider to be your ideal partner? What race, appearance or job would that person

have?

- Who do you think would be the ideal partner for you? What race, appearance, job, or interests would that person have?
- What three things stress you out or overwhelm you most? How do you cope with and manage stress?
- How do you respond/what do you do when you feel angry? Sad?
- Do you get along with all of your friends?
- What do you think are the most important qualities of a good friend?
- Do any of your friends smoke, use drugs or alcohol?
- What is your closest/most challenging relationship right now?
- Who do you dislike most? What is the best thing about that person?
- What is a bad habit you have in your life right now? What would you like to change?
- What is your biggest challenge in life right now? What kind of support do you need to get through this challenge?
- What is the best and worst part of being a teen?
- Who do you trust most and least in your life?
- When you are having a problem in your life, who can provide you with support? Why do you feel you can trust this person?
- Who is one person who has hurt your feelings and how did you get through it?
- What do you most want to be remembered for?

Question Game With Ball

You will need a ball with the numbers 1-20 taped to its surface with transparent tape. Have everyone sit in a circle. One person starts by tossing the ball to someone in the circle.

The number facing them will have a corresponding question (see list of Council/Speed Dating questions, or the questions listed below) asked of them by the group leader.

The person who catches the ball must answer the question.

Example Questions For Question Game With Ball

- What is your favorite hobby?
- Who do you admire most?
- What is your favorite singer/band?
- What is one thing you enjoy most about your school?
- If you could go anywhere in the world, where would you go?
- What is your favorite movie?
- What is your favorite food?
- Do you prefer spending time at the beach, the mountains, or the forest?
- If you could only have one of these on a cold day, which would it be: gloves, a beanie, or a scarf?
- What's your favorite color for a car?
- Would you rather be the President of the United States or the President of Starbucks?
- If you had to choose to have either 10 cats or 10 dogs at your home, which would you choose?
- If you had to choose to have either 10 sisters or 10 brothers,

which would you choose?

- If you had to choose between being locked in a room filled to the top with dirty Kleenex or dirty socks, which would you choose?
- What is your favorite television show?
- If you had to pick one of the following, which would you choose: to jump out of an airplane with a parachute or hold on to a rope attached to a flying helicopter?
- What is your favorite sport to play and/or watch?
- Would you rather sleep all day, read all day or watch TV all day?
- What is one thing you enjoy about AHA!?
- Say one positive thing about yourself and one positive thing about someone else in the room.

People Search

Make one copy of the chart on the following page for each participant. Then, have each member of the group try to find a person who fits the description in one of the boxes. Have that person sign his or her name in the box.

If the person is required to demonstrate knowledge (for example, naming U.S. presidents), he or she must do so before signing. Depending on the size of the group, each person only fill in one or two boxes on any other player's sheet. Each participant may use him or herself in one box.

Whoever fills the whole first sheet wins. If you have time, have the winner stand in front of the group and read the name of the person who has signed within each box.

The People Search sheet can be edited to better suit the group with whom you're working.

People Search				
Has a food allergy – what is it?	Is the same age as you	Has only sisters or brothers	Has met someone famous. Who was it?	Can say hello in four different languages
Likes sushi	Has had or currently has braces	Can name the mayor of [your town]	Can pat their head and rub their stomach at the same time	Has more than one hole pierced in their ears
Has never broken a bone	Can play a musical instrument	Keeps a journal	Can whistle "Row, row, row your boat"	Was not born in [your state]
Was born the same month as you	Is an only child	Has visited more than three different states	Is left-handed	Can name five US presidents
Plays a sport	Has never flown in an airplane	Has five or more cavities	Wears glasses	Speaks a foreign language – which one?

Community-Building Games

These games are meant to give youth opportunities to feel supported, supportive, and collaborative.

Ball Challenge

Participants form a circle and pass a Koosh ball back and forth, each person making sure to remember who passed the ball to them and to whom they passed it. A passing sequence is created and memorized. In the first round, players may raise their hands when they've had a turn so as not to receive the ball twice.

Ball Challenge Variation

When the facilitator feels the group is ready, additional balls can be added to the same sequence. The group is asked to see how fast they can pass all of the balls in the same sequence, with a new ball being tossed in to the first person soon after the previous ball has left his or her hands. Challenge players to beat their best time. The only rule is that every ball must pass through each and every person's hands; in other words, they can't just stand there and hold it.

Human Knot

Participants form a circle. Each person places his or her right hand into the center of the circle. Each person grasps someone else's right hand with his or her own. Then, they do the same with the left hand. Next, the group is asked to unwind itself into a circle. This can take time and patience. Participants must not separate their hands.

Debrief with a conversation about what the youth learned about themselves in this challenging activity. Who stepped most naturally into leadership roles? How did they lead? What emotions came up and how did they manage them? Try this as a silent activity, or with the instruction that natural leaders should stay quiet to allow others to speak up.

Helium Hoop

The facilitator should break up the groups into roughly 6-10 people. The entire pod should be able to stand around a large hula hoop with one finger touching it. The facilitator will hold up the hula hoop over the heads of the participants as they stand in a circle. Their goal is to bring the hula hoop to the ground. The only rule is that every participant must have one finger touching the hula hoop at all times. If any finger loses contact with the hoop they must start over.

Participants will soon realize that this is very challenging and that the hula hoop has a tendency to continue to rise. Allow the group to work together to figure out what works best for them. Pause intermittently if needed to ask questions like, "What is working well right now? What do we need to do differently?" Once the group completes the task or can no longer stick with it ask process questions to debrief like, "What emotions came up for you during this activity? What did you notice? What role did you take in the team? What did you appreciate about the team?"

This game can bring up a lot of tension and discomfort. It is okay! Be sure to process and hear from everyone in the group so that participants leave feeling empowered and having learned something new about their group and themselves.

Organic Orchestra

Participants sit or stand in a circle. One person starts a beat. Others contribute to that beat with words, sounds, or movements until everyone in the group is rhythmically involved. The facilitator acts as a conductor, raising or lowering the volume or moving participants about in rhythm sections.

Full, Half, Fourth & Find

Participants stand in a circle and are counted off into groups of three. The facilitator begins to clap a simple, repetitive rhythm that the whole group then picks up and follows. The facilitator then directs just the 1's to follow his or her clap and tells the 2's and 3's to stop clapping. The 1's are instructed to continue on the full beat. Then, the facilitator leads the 2's to clap on the half-beat (1/2 time), which the 2's then maintain (simultaneously, as the 1's maintain their full beat). Now, the facilitator leads the 3's on the fourth beat (1/4 time) and the 3's maintain this beat. In unison, the 1's are clapping on the full beat, the 2's on the half-beat and the 3's on the fourth-beat.

Full, Half, Fourth & Find Variations

- The facilitator asks for a volunteer to clap a simple beat. All the 1's follow the volunteer's beat. All 2's join in on the half-beat. All 3's join in on the fourth-beat. If the group has trouble, the leader can count out the beats (1,2,3,4) so participants can follow along more easily.

- The facilitator becomes the conductor. Just the 1's...just 2's...just 3's...now, mix them up, adding 1's and 2's together...adding 2's and 3's, etc. Then, in unison again, everyone claps his or her assigned beat.

- The conductor can direct the group to move out of the circle and mingle while clapping continues. Then, without talking, participants find their group by recognizing the clap that matches their own.

Freeze Tag

The player chosen as "It" holds an object that shows that he or she is the one to run from. (A rubber chicken is always good fun.) When the person designated "it" tags another person, that person becomes "frozen." Two people can release a frozen player by creating a circle around him or her with their arms and chanting "You're free!" three times. That person is then unfrozen – free to continue playing and to help others get free.

Appreciation Tag

Choose one to two players as "It." Players who are tagged are frozen. To unfreeze a fellow player, another player must touch him or her and give an appreciation.

AHA! wishes to express gratitude to Isis Castaneda, Brent Blair, Mitchell Torena (of the Camp Whittier Ropes Course) and William Gale for sharing these exercises and teaching us to masterfully facilitate them.

Council Circle

Teenagers need to be heard, and they need to learn to value the art of listening. Council has proven the best way to tap into both individual and collective expression from program participants. It is central to the AHA! Method.

Council has been practiced across times and cultures all over the world. This method comes to us through generations of indigenous practices of problem-solving and storytelling. It entails structured individual sharing as part of a group that is seated in a circle. Participants sit with others, using a talking piece (an object that confers the right to speak without interruption) to allow for unfettered sharing and deep listening.

Council teaches us to learn collectively, prizing the resources of each person rather than over-valuing specific individual contributions from those considered more "cool" or popular by peers. It teaches that the role of the witness – the person who simply listens and empathizes with the person speaking – is as important as the role of the speaker.

Silence is embraced in council as a valid contribution. A participant holding the talking piece is regarded as the speaker even when he or she does not utter a word. In this way, we teach and learn that each person deserves attention for his or her living presence. A respect for all varied forms of experience and expression is cultivated. Council circle strategies bring the vitality of every participant into the classroom or educational setting.

Council can be used to connect people who don't know one another; as a way to address important issues or get everyone's voice in the room regarding a topic that matters; or as a way to repair harm done within a classroom or program community.

Council Guidelines

Council can be used to open or close AHA! sessions. Council can also be called at any time during a session, or to mark the end of a series of sessions to foster closure and closeness.

Begin by ceremonializing the center of the circle with beautiful or meaningful objects that help honor the importance of the gathering. Allow a participant to dedicate that day's council to anything or anyone he or she chooses. Participants love to dedicate councils to friends, family or ideas. Light a candle to bring focus to and honor the intention as it is stated. At the end of the council, have the same person restate the intention and blow out the candle as a distinct completion ritual.

Council Agreements

No matter what type of council is held, these four elements must always be honored by those who share:

1. Speak from the heart.
2. Listen from the heart without prejudgment.
3. Keep it lean – express what you need to and remember the needs of others to speak.
4. Be spontaneous – don't rehearse what you will say or do when the talking piece comes to you; the magic comes from speaking or act from your heart in that moment, without preparation.
5. Keep the privacy of the circle. Do not share about what was said in the circle unless you wish to share something about your own contribution.

Topics for Council

93

Council topics can run the gamut of fun and silly to serious and deep.

General Questions

- Share about your name. What does it mean?
- Who were you named after?
- Do you like your name?
- Do you have any nicknames?
- What is one thing about yourself that most people do not know?
- Tell about a time when you felt peer pressure. What was it about? What did you do?
- Tell about a time when you felt lucky.
- Tell about a time when you felt everything was going wrong.
- Tell about the world you would like to live in.
- What are some stereotypes you have about boys?
- What are some stereotypes you have about girls?
- How do you want to be treated by the opposite sex?
- What are some of your fears about being a teen?
- Share a recurring dream you have had.
- What are your thoughts on death?
- What experiences have you had with the death of family, friends, or pets?

Trust

- Who do you trust in your life?
- If you had a personal problem in your life, whom would you

talk to? What is it about this person that makes you trust them?

- How does it feel to be trusted? Tell about a time when someone trusted you.
- Tell a story about a time when someone you trusted betrayed you. What happened to your trust?
- Tell a story about a time when you betrayed a trust.
- What are the signs that tell you when you are becoming distrustful? What makes a good friend?
- What makes a bad friend?

Cliques, Safety and Trust

- What is a clique? What do you call such a group?
- Do you have cliques in your school?
- Why are some people more popular than others?
- If you are in a clique, what makes you feel good about it?
- Tell about a time when you felt left out. How did you feel? What actions did you take?
- Why do we need to feel accepted?
- Share a time when you went out of your way to show acceptance and include someone else.

Laughing With vs. Laughing At

- Share your most embarrassing moment.
- Share a time when you were laughed at and how it felt.
- Share the first family reunion you ever went to.
- Share the worst gift you ever received or gave someone.
- What is the difference between laughing at a funny story and laughing at a person? (Laughing with vs. laughing at)

Building Community

- Tell about a time when you were not listened to. How did it feel? What did you do?
- Tell about a time when you couldn't do something by yourself and reached out for help in a way you hadn't before.
- What makes you angry?
- Share something you really like about yourself.
- Share about a time when someone really made a change or difference in your life.
- Share about someone who really inspires you.
- Share about a time when you felt disrespected. What was that like?
- Share how you think the group can have more respect for one another.

Personality

- If you could describe your personality as a kind of shoe…which would it be and why? Ballet shoe, football shoe, soccer cleat, tennis shoe, mountain climber shoe, baby shoe, clown shoe…
- If you could describe your personality as a type of hat…a musical instrument…an animal…a flower…a food…what would it be?

Male and Female

- Have boys sit in outer circle; girls in inner circle. Each circle should be facing the center of the circle.
- Suggest a topic or question: What is it that you want the other sex to know about you? What do you love most about

being male? Being female?

- After the inner circle answers the questions, switch so that the inner circle becomes the outer circle and answers the same questions.

Open Council

When there is a sense of the council question or topic becoming muddled or is not really tapping into the core essence of participants, facilitators may ask to change the existing direction or theme of the council by calling for an Open Council. As youth learn about the Council process, they can also be empowered to make this same call where they see fit.

At this point, any facilitator or participant can ask, "What needs to change in order to make this a more potent and relevant council?" The group then uses the talking piece to share ideas about how to improve the direction or theme of the circle. This can be an empowering choice that deepens self- awareness and ability to process as a group.

Connection Circles

Research shows that the most effective way to decrease prejudice and build peaceful, connected community is through face-to-face, meaningful interaction. It's not enough just to sit next to someone in class or to make small talk at lunchtime.

Connection Circles are a simplified form of Council Circle that AHA! uses to quickly and easily create a forum for this kind of interaction, free of interruptions and distractions. They help prevent bullying and cruel behavior among youth by providing a strong container for building empathy.

Connection Circles follow a simplified format that can be learned and led by virtually anyone. As is the case with all Council Circles, these require a commitment to one person speaking at a time, and to cultivating a safe space where every person's voice matters.

They can be held with anywhere from two to 30 or more people. For elementary-aged children, ideal group size is 6-8; junior high and high school Connection Circles ideally involve 8-15 participants.

Setting Up Connection Circles

Choose a talking piece. Anything can be used, but it's nice to have something special. Children love to make their own talking pieces.

As with Council, you may wish to create a ceremonial/ritual environment different from ordinary conversational environments. You might light a candle and dedicate the circle if time permits. If this is not possible, the leader can create a similar environment by reading the Connection Circle guidelines to the group with purpose:

Connection Circle Guidelines

Connection Circles are run according to five guidelines similar to those of Council Circle.

1. **Speak from your heart.** *Speak your truth without mentally rehearsing.*
2. **Listen deeply with respect.** *Listening from the heart is about*

being willing to not have any prefixed notion of what the person will say;
about listening to others with total attention and using the opportunity
to see and hear them as exactly who they are.

3. **Be spontaneous.** *Don't rehearse what you will say while others are speaking.*

4. **Be mindful of time.** *Every person needs to have time to speak.*

5. **Keep the privacy of the circle.** *What is shared in the circle stays in the circle.*

After sharing these guidelines with participants, the facilitator asks for a thumbs-up or head nod indicating agreement to uphold them.

Facilitator then states the topic and responds to the topic first. "So, now that we all agree on the guidelines, today we'll be talking about 'x'. The first question is…" Once the question is posed, the facilitator answers first to set the tone.

It is very important that the facilitator speaks honestly, vulnerably, and briefly, without inappropriate self-disclosure. You are setting the norm for the rest of the circle.

After sharing, the talking piece is passed to the left. After each person has spoken and the talking piece has arrived back with the facilitator, the facilitator summarizes what was said in the circle, naming any themes that were evident. He or she then states the next topic and passes to the left once again.

Participants can pass; the fact that they hold the piece and pass it means they are included in the circle.

Start off by making sure everybody has a comfortable seat. Let them know that it is perfectly OK to stretch and move and change their positions – to have comfort in their physical body in order to listen.

Check-Ins

It is good for the first topic of every circle to be some kind of check-in. It helps to see what's going on in the students' lives and how they are doing that day.

Our favorite is Thorns and Roses, described in detail in previous sections. Other check-ins described in that section will also work well in the Connection Circle format.

Suitable Connection Circle Questions

Choose questions that are open-ended (not yes/no) and elicit thoughtful sharing, not judgment or a 'performance' designed to try to impress others.

Example: "Name a time you felt truly successful in something that you put a lot of effort into."

As the facilitator, I would answer first, sharing something like: "The time we held a conference for 200 student Peace Builders and watched them conduct their own Connection Circles, which they had learned to do from a previous training." Then, I would pass the talking piece and others would answer in turn.

Other examples of good Connection Circle questions are below. Some are serious; others, more light-hearted and fun. As you gain experience with Circle leadership, you will develop an instinct for choosing the right kinds of questions for whatever group you find gathered with you.

- Name a time that you felt excluded. What was that like?
- Name a time that you felt included. What was that like?
- What can you do to be more inclusive toward others?
- Who is a role model for you and why?
- Tell about a person in your life who you didn't think you liked or loved, but who taught you something important.
- Share about a place or time where you felt a lack of confidence.
- Share about a place or a time where you felt a lot of confidence.
- What interrupts our confidence? How do we regroup when we fail?
- If you could have a soundtrack to your life, what would be the intro song?
- If you were stranded on a desert island, what three items would you choose to have with you?
- If you could have any heightened sense, what would it be?
- If you could either walk on water or breathe under water, what would you choose? Why?
- During a natural disaster, what three items would you grab right away?
- Who would you want to play you in a movie? Why?
- If you were to be a leader of a nation, would you want the biggest army or the biggest educational budget? Why?
- What is the cleverest thing you have ever gotten away with?
- If karma were to bite you in the butt, what would it do to you?

- What is the most private thing you are willing to admit?
- What was your worst date, ever?
- What is the silliest thing you did as a kid?
- If you had to be named another name, what would you call yourself?
- If you were one article of clothing, what would you be? Why?
- Describe your first crush.
- Describe the most beautiful thing you have ever seen.
- If you were immortal for a day, what would you do?
- If you had to be the other gender, who would you be? Why?
- What's your superhero name?
- If you had a time machine that would work only once, what point in the future or history would you visit?
- If you could talk to any one person now living, who would it be and why?
- If I gave you $10,000, what would you spend it on?

In a Connection Circle, as with any Council Circle, there is no back and forth, interruption, or competition for the floor. Connection Circles are held in an environment where others can be heard without distraction, and without food, drink, or digital devices.

In our culture of extroversion, Connection Circles are a simple, reliable way to create a true democracy of voice. Connection Circles offer relief from needing to have our voice matter more than someone else's. They give an opportunity to shy, reluctant speakers to feel heard in equal standing for perhaps the first time. Always keep in mind that Connection Circle leadership is characterized by curiosity and humor. It is not judgmental or heavy-handed. As leader, always remember that everyone is doing his or her best in the moment.

Part Four

Creating Closure in the AHA!

Method

Creating Closure in the AHA! Method

How a group ends is just as important as how one has begun. Whether in an individual group session or across a series of sessions over a period of time, participants may have opened their hearts and shared personal secrets and truths. At the very least, they feel a sense of connection that is important and brings vulnerability. It is important to honor this vulnerability by closing individual sessions or series of sessions with reverence.

Conscious completion in the AHA! Method helps participants begin to make more conscious choices as to how they personally wish to have closure in their own lives and worlds. It helps youth to see that being present while preparing to part ways is as important as looking toward the future and moving toward what's next.

First, let's look at some ideas for closing individual sessions; we will then look at ways AHA! closes groups that have been together over a period of time.

Concluding Individual Sessions

Concluding a group meeting necessitates a time for review, reflection and completion of what has transpired. It's an opportunity to review the overall tone or energy of the group and reflect upon specific interactions or occurrences.
AHA! wishes to acknowledge and appreciate Cindy Carter, Dave Newcomer, Brent Blair, and William Gale for contributing the exercises in this section.

Facilitation Tips and Objectives: Closing Sessions

Ensure that all participants have the opportunity to speak prior to completing the session.

Invite sharing via questions, concerns and feedback.

Reiterate the agreement to confidentiality and acknowledge both those who have shared and those who have listened, particularly when deep sharing has occurred.

Facilitators should help sum up the experiences of the day in positive frames. For example: "Today, we have been challenged by a few conflicts. We have each had to learn about patience, openness and authenticity. I think we have all gained more understanding about the importance of seeing a conflict through."

Facilitating a game or exercise that initiates movement and fun (before the final circle) provides the opportunity to end on a high note and/or shift the energy of the group. This is particularly useful when it has been a more didactic and/or thought-provoking session where participants have been sitting for a long period of time. It is especially helpful to ask participants which game they would like to play as a closing game.

The facilitator should use all that has transpired in the group as inspiration for further work and as material to use for acknowledging group participation and group gains. Youth can participate in closing by sharing something that stood out about the day's activities or something they don't wish to leave unsaid.

Closing Exercises, Games, and Activities For Individual Sessions

Appreciation/gratitude circles.

Part of living a balanced life is to be aware of and to acknowledge what we give to others as well as what we have received. Appreciation circles are a way to reflect upon and acknowledge beginnings and endings with a spirit of gratitude. They help us remember our essence and the effects we cause in our lives. Having this reflected back to us by peers is nourishing and often a powerful reminder of who we really are.

For the facilitator: Invite all participants to express their gratitude to facilitators, especially when a visiting facilitator is present. Participants are invited to appreciate what the facilitator has brought to the group in personal terms – how the facilitator has affected them directly or what they specifically liked about the lesson presented.

- For the group: Occasionally (usually after the group has been together for some time), we will ask the participants how this group is affecting their lives. What are they thankful for? Why? Going around the circle, everyone has the opportunity to speak as they wish.

- For each other: Going around the circle, each member receives three or four appreciations from individual participants in the group. Participants express appreciation by choice – there is no obligation. This activity can be divided up into two rounds, where the first round is expressing gratitude for what the member has positively contributed to the group, and a second round as an appreciation for who they are – the attributes others admire about their essence.

- Word rally: All participants form a tight circle. Each participant is invited to call out a one- word feeling about the group. Words bubble up and gather in speed and volume, creating a pep chorus: "Happy...Cool...Grateful..." As momentum gains, words spring out faster and more expressively.

Check-Out

Participants form a circle. Using a talking piece, give each participant an opportunity to speak before the group closes. The principles of council are observed. The leader may ask prompting questions or give guidance about what to share.

Some examples:

- What did you like the least in group today?
- What did you like the most?
- What are you taking with you from the group today?
- What are you looking forward to this week?

Depending upon how much time the group has been together, what has occurred in the group and the time remaining, check-out can take on many forms. It can be playful and silly or serious and heartfelt. The secret is to gauge what the group needs in the moment, and to wrap up by meeting those needs.

Commitment Circle

All participants form a tight circle so that everyone is standing, facing to the right. Left hands are placed in the middle of the circle, giving the "thumbs up." Then the thumbs go sideways so that each participant holds the thumb of the person behind him or her, forming an inner circle where everyone is connected. Depending upon what has occurred earlier, the leader may choose various themes with which to close. For example: "We have now formed a commitment circle where we all commit to holding what has happened here today in confidentiality. In agreeing to this, each person says their name around the circle." Or: "We have now formed a commitment circle where we have all agreed to treat one another with trust and respect. In agreeing to this, each person says their name around the circle."

Thorns and Roses

This exercise can be used to check in or check out of a group meeting.

Can you spare a compliment?

For this activity, you'll need a stack of 3x5 index cards. For a larger group, you might need full sheets of paper.

1. Each participant writes his or her name on an index card and passes it back to the leader, who shuffles and redistributes the cards so that no one has the card with his/her own name on it.
2. Each person then writes something that they like or a compliment about that person under his/her name. No jokes – it has to be a true compliment.
3. Each person passes the card back to the leader without

signing it.

4. Re-shuffle and repeat the number of times necessary for all cards to go to all participants.

5. When done, the cards should be collected and read out loud. The facilitator should ensure that each description is positive and appropriate; replace anything negative or inappropriate with a true compliment.

6. The person complimented should only say "Thank you."

Pass the Hug

Self-explanatory! Have participants stand in a circle. One person volunteers to go first. He or she passes a hug to the next person in the circle. The hug continues around the whole circle.

Self-Love

Participants stand in a circle. One by one, they share one nice thing they've done for themselves or wanted to do for themselves in the past week. Have them share how good self-care feels.

Completion: Facilitation Tips and Activities

The following tips are for wrapping up groups that have been together for a while and have developed a deep bond over multiple meetings.

Begin to acknowledge the coming completion of the program at least one week before its end. Prior to the last meeting, during council/check-in, ask how people are feeling about the program or class coming to its finish. Use participants' feedback to begin gauging and preparing your activities. Inquire about how participants intend to support themselves after the group is finished. If any participant seems especially upset about the group ending, offer ideas for finding emotional support. Where appropriate, make a realistic, concrete follow-up plan with each participant.

Group Letter to Everyone

Bring special paper and good pens for everyone present. Every person writes his or her name at the top of a piece of paper. Each paper is then passed around the circle so that each participant can write something heartfelt on each group member's paper. When completed, each participant will receive this personal memento. With a large group, this can take an entire group meeting, but is a wonderful way to close.

Predictions

The group makes positive predictions about where each member of the group will be in ten years: what they will be doing, where they will be living, and whom they will be with. The group takes a moment to think about each person in the circle, one at a time, and offers its prediction to the group and to the person directly.

Council

Wrapping-up activities can include council circles or Connection Circles. Revisit the topics listed in the sections on Council and Connection Circles.

Appreciation Circle

The group sits in circle. Going around, each member receives three or four appreciations from the group. This can be divided into two rounds: the first round expresses gratitude for what the member has contributed to the group or what he or she has done that has been beneficial to the group. The second round is an appreciation for who the person is – the attributes that the others admire about their essence.

Party

A party gives everyone a chance to have fun together and to release any residual energy left over from final, formal closing rituals.

Postcards

Each participant writes a postcard to every other participant about what they will miss about that person. The facilitators then take these postcards and mail groups of them throughout the year so that participants feel their connection extending over time.

Giveaway Ceremony

All participants (not including facilitators) bring something with personal significance with which they are willing to permanently part.

The items are placed on a special blanket in the center of the circle. Facilitators should not know who brought each item, so shouldn't watch participants placing items in the circle's center.

In silence, the group sits in a circle around the blanket.

Facilitators then view all the items and direct each person to choose the item she or he is drawn to. If someone is undecided, encourage her or him to be intuitive about which item's attraction is stronger. Participants should remain in silence.

After choosing an item, each participant sits sit back in the circle.

Once everyone has chosen, each giver locates the person who chose his or her item.

The receiving person tells the giving member what it was that attracted him or her to the item and why this item seems to have significance.

The giving member then tells the recipient what meaning and importance that item has had for them. A sense of commonality is often felt through this exchange, deepening personal connection.

This activity works when the program has begun with facilitators giving away to youth at the first or second session. The closing give-away to facilitators is a completion and expression of gratitude at the end.

Thank You

This wild vision of AHA! was conceived to build a community of loving, wise teenagers – teens willing to reach beyond themselves to care about others and about their communities.

Thank you for showing up to help these strong roots grow deeper.

About the Creators of AHA!

Jennifer Freed, Ph.D., MFT, and Rendy Freedman, MFT, co-founders and co-directors of AHA!, bring over 40 years of combined experience working with young people. Freed was the director of a statewide media project for teenagers and Freedman was one of the founders of the Waldorf School in Santa Barbara.

Both are licensed family therapists, psychology professors, educators, and trained mediators. Dr. Freed is a recognized expert on matters such as teen bullying, character development, marriage and family relationships, and diversity appreciation.

She was the clinical director at Pacifica Graduate Institute, where she continues to serve as a professor and workshop leader. She created the teen and young adult workbook series *Become Your Best Self,* which includes workbooks on *Relationship Wisdom, Character, Compassion* and *Creative Expression,* and a book based in AHA!'s Peace Builders work with youth, PeaceQ.

AHA! won the Best Santa Barbara Local Youth Agency award in 2010; the workbooks Dr. Freed created won the prestigious Hope Award; and in 2014, AHA!'s out-of-school program was selected as one of the eight top social-emotional learning out-of-school programs in the U.S. by the Susan Crown Exchange.

Through SCE, AHA! participated in developing a best-practices manual for integrating social-emotional learning (SEL) into out-of-school programs, and is involved in ongoing efforts to train youth providers on using the SCE's SEL Field Guide in tandem with the AHA! Method. The manual can be accessed at https://www.selpractices.org.

Jennifer Freed (left) and Rendy Freedman (right)

Made in the USA
San Bernardino, CA
27 August 2017